THE SPARKLE OF HIS EYE

THE SPARKLE OF HIS EYE

Discovering Beauty in the Broken

Stefani A. Weatherford

ELM HILL

A Division of
HarperCollins Christian Publishing

www.elmhillbooks.com

The Sparkle of His Eye

Discovering Beauty in the Broken

Published in Nashville, Tennessee, by Elm Hill, an imprint of Thomas Nelson. Elm Hill and Thomas Nelson are registered trademarks of HarperCollins Christian Publishing, Inc.

Elm Hill titles may be purchased in bulk for educational, business, fund-raising, or sales promotional use. For information, please e-mail SpecialMarkets@ ThomasNelson.com.

Library of Congress Cataloging-in-Publication Data

Library of Congress Control Number: 2019910015

ISBN 978-1-400325665 (Paperback)
ISBN 978-1-400325672 (eBook)

CONTENTS

FOREWORD

. . .

I don't usually remember my dreams, but occasionally I'll have one that leaves an impression. Usually it's the scary ones where I wake up in a panic and am thankful when I realize it was just a dream. But on this particular evening, I had a funny dream. I think I may have even laughed myself awake. All I remember is that I was in a room full of family and friends, and I had just shared the news that I had gotten engaged. I'm not even sure whom my fiancé was, but I had a bright, sparkly ring on my finger, and they gasped in shock at the news.

I started cracking up at their response and just remember muttering through my laughter, "That's so funny you guys are so surprised someone wants to marry me again!" I realize now as I write that, it is more sad than funny that my mind would immediately interpret their gasp negatively rather than them being happy for me. If I'm being completely honest, it does cross my mind that people probably wonder what's wrong with me that I've been single this long since my divorce. When I get in that mind-set, it hurts deeply. Every woman wants to feel like she is wanted, loved and enough. It's hard to feel those things when years go by and you're still alone.

I woke up about midnight and couldn't shake that dream. The words "Twinkle, Twinkle" stuck in my mind. I knew I always wanted to write a book one day to bring purpose to my pain, but I didn't understand what those two words had to do with any of it.

Then my mind flashed to the ring. One of the things I loved most about my ring was how sparkly it was. Often the twinkle of the light reflecting off the diamond just right would catch my attention. I realize when I start these next few sentences, you might think I'm superficial, but hear me out…

One of the hardest parts of divorce for me was taking off my ring. When I got married, I thought I could cross that off my bucket list. I thought I was done with the searching and waiting phase and was excited to have my person to grow old with. He had chosen me. We were a family. And families are forever…or at least I thought they were.

It turns out, he made it seem as if I was easily replaced. One time I asked him what she had that I didn't and in one word he disqualified all of the years I tried to be the best wife I could be. He looked me straight in the face and said, "Everything."

Everything.

That encompasses so much. He didn't just list a few good qualities she had that he preferred or even the things about me he'd wish I'd change. In that moment, in his mind, she was everything to him that I wasn't.

The most miserable six months of my life were living with a man who loved another woman. No matter how hard I tried or fought for our marriage, he was already gone. His heart was taken. Snatched right out of my grasp without me getting a say. No matter how many hours we spent in counseling or talking through our issues, no matter how many tears I cried, I couldn't win him back.

The day I took off my ring was Divorce Day for me. I didn't need a judge to make it official. The choice was already made, and it wasn't me. As I slid my ring off of my finger, reality set in. My "for better or worse" became less than seven years. My happily ever after was given to someone else. I was replaced. I wasn't enough.

The diamond itself was beautiful, and yes, it made me smile when I admired it, but it was what it symbolized that meant the world to me. It meant I was taken. I was chosen by someone who wanted to spend the rest of their life with me. Out of all of the girlfriends, I made the cut and advanced to wife material. I was loved. I was enough.

Since I no longer had the sparkle on my finger, I had to find it inside of myself. I was a wreck emotionally, and it was starting to affect me physically. I knew I couldn't live that way. I needed to do something, but I wasn't quite sure what. And so my journey began, and in time, I pieced together seven key elements that I needed in order to be able to shine again.

I pray that you'll take this journey with me with an open heart and open mind. Whether you've gone through a divorce or another kind of heart break, my hope is that you will find something that speaks to your heart and inspires you to not just survive but to live life to the fullest.

At the end of each section, there are questions to consider. I encourage you to find a small group to journey with as you read. My hope is that this brings together those in different phases of the healing process so you can learn and grow together. I envision a start line and finish line with people lined up at the different mile markers. As you connect, you join hands and help each other through to the next milestone.

"A person standing alone can be attacked and defeated, but two can stand back-to-back and conquer. Three are even better, for a triple-braided cord is not easily broken."
— ECCLESIASTES 4:12, NLT

STRENGTH

. . .

December 31ˢᵗ – Packing day.

I had to muster up every last bit of strength that I had in order to pack up and move from our home where I had planned to raise our son and into our new apartment. I had spent all of that fall fighting for my marriage, digging my heels in and refusing to let go. When I realized that he was going to be with her whether I liked it or not and flaunt it in front of my face, I decided it was time to move on.

I was out of strength and I needed a new beginning. I didn't want to be the bitter woman that I was becoming. Anger took over often as I struggled alone in my circumstances while trying to be strong for my little one. I was beginning to despise the person I saw in the mirror, and my stress was beginning to affect our son. I had to protect him. I needed a safe place to mend my broken heart, and so we moved out.

It had been almost seven years since I had lived alone. There were many nights that I was scared, but I couldn't be because I had to be brave for my son. I had also never lived in an apartment before, and realization sunk in that it wasn't just my decisions I had to worry about. I'd lay in bed at night and pray that my neighbors made safe choices so that we never had to experience something tragic like a fire.

Even though I had taken the first steps of moving on, I didn't want my marriage to be over. My ex would give me glimpses of hope, and so I was attached to an emotional yo-yo for all of that year. Talk about draining! Many mornings, it took everything I had to get out of bed. Between the crying and countless hours spent wondering how I was going to do this all on my own, I was beyond exhausted. I still had an active 3-year-old at this point to take care of and a full-time job that demanded my time.

I somehow managed to get us dressed and out the door. Once I was in my car and had dropped off my son, I'd turn on "A Little Bit Stronger" by Sara Evans and sing my heart out. If I was feeling feisty, I'd follow that with "The Best Days of Your Life" by Kellie Pickler and smirk a little. I'd cry all the way to work, dry my eyes in the parking lot and put a smile on my face. I didn't want to let everyone know what was going on because I still had hope we could work this out.

I thought once we were gone that he'd realize how incomplete he felt and ask us to come back home. My hopeless romantic self would envision him standing at my apartment door with flowers and his apology speech all prepared. But day after day, I'd round the corner to the apartment breezeway to find no one was there. He never came for us.

I began to realize quickly that I needed something more than my own strength. I needed to go back to church. I had always loved how I felt when I went to my church that I had been going to for years off and on. There was just something special that I felt when I was there that I couldn't quite put my finger on.

I'd sit in the worship experience and ball my eyes out. Every word touched my spirit in ways that I couldn't explain. I felt a certain comfort and peace when I was in the sanctuary that gave me hope. I clung to every word of the message as I scribbled my notes. I'd write down every Scripture that spoke to me, and before long, I had post-its throughout my entire apartment to encourage me.

"The Lord is near to those who are discouraged; he saves those who have lost all hope."

– *PSALM 34:18, GNT*

"He heals the broken-hearted and bandages their wounds."
– PSALM 147:3, GNT

"Trust in the Lord with all your heart and lean not on your own understanding; in all your ways submit to him, and he will make your paths straight."
– PROVERBS 3:5-6, NIV

I'd even post Scripture in dry erase markers on our bathroom mirrors to remind us that we weren't alone and we didn't need to be afraid. I took Bible study classes and bought Veggie Tale DVD's for my son so we could immerse ourselves in God's Word in every way. I needed to soak in His Presence in order to make it through another week. There were some days I wish I could hide in the sanctuary after service and live there. I needed to feel His Presence every day. Slowly but surely, I began strengthening my spirit so that I could feel Him with me always.

. . . .

Once the divorce was final, part of me was so embarrassed. I now had the "divorced" label, and every time I filled out a form from that day forward, I had to check "that" box. But I couldn't let this failure define me. Yes, I went through a divorce, but that doesn't determine who I am as a person or my future.

"It's in developing a relationship with your weakness and your fail-ures that your greatest opportunity for growth exists." (Furtick 2016)

I fought the divorce with every ounce of my being. I didn't like being in that weak, vulnerable state. Feeling so out of control of my life was unsettling. At first, I let my state of weakness govern my life. I let it con-sume my mind and allow it to cause me to make irrational decisions. I let my emotions take over my spirit and very quickly realized this was no way to live.

Once I began a relationship with the Lord, I finally began to focus on Him which created a stability and strength deep within that I could not explain. It took a while, but I'd slowly notice that a few days would pass without me crying. My analytical mind tried making sense of this new-found strength, but it was impossible.

Throughout the next few years, I would learn that this strength was not in me but outside of Him, it was only *through* Him that I had strength. For example, I'd start feeling stronger and then I'd venture off to conquer more. But if I relied on my own strength, I quickly became weak. I had to remain in Him – meaning a daily walk, coming before Him and surrendering my will for His. It was a process of giving to God and then often taking back. But that's one of the things that made me fall in love with the Lord because He's so sweet in the way He loves us.

No matter how many times I'd try to take back control, He was always there when I'd fall on my knees begging for help again. He was always faithful. Never changing. The same today, tomorrow, and always. He was the stability I needed. Even though I was like a toddler gripping the ball in a tantrum when things didn't go my way, He'd patiently wait until I was ready to release it back into His hands. Like a sweet, patient Daddy smiling down on His little girl and encouraging me every time I followed His lead like, "There you go my girl, I'm proud of you for taking this step. Keep trusting and I promise I will never fail you or forsake you."

I had been forsaken. The *one* person who promised to love me until the day he died changed his mind. But God said He would *never* forsake me. When I heard that, I clung to that Word like an anchor. It took me some time to believe it, but God is just as much patient as he is faithful.

And so, this gem right here helped me understand the source of my strength–the first key element in restoring my luster...

"But He said to me, "My grace is sufficient for you, for my power is made perfect in weakness." Therefore, I will boast all the more gladly about my weaknesses, so that Christ's power may rest on me. That is why, for Christ's sake, I delight in weaknesses, in insults, in hardships, in persecutions, in difficulties. For when I am weak, then I am strong."

– 2 CORINTHIANS 12:9-11, NIV

You might be wondering what a daily walk with the Lord looks like. If I could relate it to something maybe more familiar, it's similar to a daily exercise routine. Unless you are already used to doing push-ups, you probably can't drop down and give me fifty without stopping. So, you'd start with ten and do that every day. As your muscles strengthen, it becomes easier to do more in a row and before you know it, you're flying through fifteen, then thirty, and so on. Each day you feel stronger.

So you start reading the verse of the day on your Bible app and listening to Kari Jobe radio station on Pandora. You set aside time throughout the day to just talk to Him. And then some quiet time to try and listen. After all, a conversation works both ways. Before you know it, you will cherish those moments when you can get alone with Him and let Him minister to your heart.

. . . .

I felt like all I did was pray in the beginning. At first, I had so much to say. I was full of hope and ready for the good fight. I truly believed that God was going to save my marriage. But then months would pass by and we were still in the same place. I'd get so discouraged and weary that I didn't even know what more to pray.

I remember one night in particular just sobbing in my shower. The bathroom had become my peaceful escape to regain my sanity. But this night, I couldn't tell the difference between my tears and the puddle of hot water falling all around me. Much like the scene described below from Beth Moore's *Whispers of Hope* devotional.

Imagine this poignant scene. The child of God musters her last bit of strength to collapse before the throne of God. Words do not come – just groanings. They are not her groanings, though they emerge from so deep within, she thinks they are hers. The Spirit of God searches her heart, gathers her pain, and lifts it to the Father of all comfort. The Spirit of God, knowing both the depth of her agony and the will of the Father, can bring forth glory from even this. He insists that the Father usher overflowing comfort. He urges the child to let the Father have His way. He prays for things she could not bear to pray – that she lacks the courage to pray. He prays for glory.

How long does the child lay before God's throne? Until strength comes. Until she identifies the heart of the Spirit's intercession for her and can make it her own. Perhaps this is one of life's finest hours for the believer – when the will of the Father and the will of the child converge as one – and the cloudy pillar of God's glory settles on her shoulders like a down comforter. And just for a moment, heaven comes to earth." (Moore 2013)

Beautiful! So beautiful! I can't even count the number of moments I had just like this. But in *every single one*, the Lord picked me up and set my feet back on solid ground. I had to realize that God couldn't save my marriage without two willing parties. I was so ready for God to calm the storm happening around me. But instead, He wanted me to find Him in the midst of it first.

. . . .

Other verses:

"The LORD is my strength and my defense; he has become my salvation. He is my God, and I will praise him, my father's God, and I will exalt him."

– *EXODUS 15:2, NIV*

"The Lord is my strength and my shield; my heart trusts in Him, and He helps me. My heart leaps for joy, and with my song I praise Him."

– PSALM 28:7, NIV

"Come to me, all you who are weary and burdened, and I will give you rest. Take my yoke upon you and learn from me, for I am gentle and humble in heart, and you will find rest for your souls. For my yoke is easy and my burden is light."

– MATTHEW 11:28-30, NIV

♪ *Song: "In My Arms" by Plumb*

Music was such a big part of my healing process! After each section, I offer a song suggestion that you might also find comfort in. As you listen, let the words settle deep in your spirit. Some will be like a love song the Lord is singing over you, and some will light a fire of inspiration deep inside.

Small Group – Session 1

Strength

1. Describe a time in your life when you needed a new beginning.
   - ❖ How long did it take you to decide that your current situation wasn't working?
   - ❖ Who did you turn to for help?
   - ❖ How did you find the strength?
   - ❖ How has your life changed since?
   - ❖ If you realize you need a new beginning but you haven't taken the first steps, consider this:
     - ✄ Is my current situation a danger to myself or my children? If yes, seek help immediately.
     - ✄ Do I have the finances to make this change? If not, how can I save money so that I have a plan?
     - ✄ Who is my support system that I can trust to offer advice that aligns with God's truth?
2. What are the warning signs of diminishing strength for you? For me, I become physically exhausted and just want to sleep.
3. What types of things make you feel strong (reading Scripture, a song/movie that inspires you)? How can you make sure you are incorporating these things into your week?
4. Are you currently involved in a church? If not, do you know someone who is that can get you plugged in? Doing life together with safe people is key to your success!
5. Which Scripture speaks to your heart about allowing God to be your strength? There are so many, it doesn't have to be one that I listed. I encourage you to pick your favorites and post them around the house.

6. What failure label have you given yourself? Sometimes we don't even realize that we have, but if you think back to the "self-talk" conversations in your mind, what negative words have you bullied yourself with? Watch Rock Thomas's "The Power of Your Identity" Goalcast on YouTube.

7. What is something you once viewed as a weakness that you can turn into a strength?

PROVISION

. . .

O ne of my first thoughts after I moved out and looked at my bank
statement was, "Oh goodness, how am I going to do this on my
own?!" My ex liked new things, so I had inherited his Jeep Commander
after he decided to buy a Mercedes that we couldn't afford. There was no
way I could pay $500+/month for a car payment, so that was the first
thing that had to go. I had gotten spoiled driving SUV's, but it was back to
a car I went. Cheaper payment. Cheaper insurance. Cheaper gas. It wasn't
as much of an adjustment as I thought, so I was happy.

Cable was another luxury that had to go. Internet was a necessity for
work, but there was no way I was spending a ridiculous amount of money
that I didn't have to watch TV. Netflix worked just fine for our needs, as I
rarely had time to sit down anyway. The last of that bundle was my phone
– we didn't need a house phone and thankfully, I had gotten a promotion
at work that provided a company phone.

My parents have always been a big help, but my dad had lost his job
in January, so they were struggling as well. I knew they would give me the
very last dollar they had, but I had to figure this out on my own. Or so I
initially thought…

So I'm sitting in church, and they start talking about tithing. I didn't
grow up understanding the concept, so this was all new to me. But so
much of my life was up in the air, that if God promised to pour out

blessings if I tested Him in this area, then by gosh I was going to test Him! I had nothing to lose and everything to gain. But I only had $15 that day. So I started with that.

> *"Bring the whole tithe into the storehouse, that there may be food in my house. Test me in this," says the LORD Almighty, "and see if I will not throw open the floodgates of heaven and pour out so much blessing that there will not be room enough to store it."*
>
> *– MALACHI 3:10, NIV*

Each week, I'd give a little more, and a little more. And faithfully, I'd watch as God placed people in my life that blessed me. Whether it was someone buying my lunch or getting $20 from someone just to help out, I could see the blessings coming. Sure enough, when I was giving almost 10% of my income (tithe = tenth), I was given another promotion at work. And it wasn't just a small promotion. It was a $10k salary bump. Coincidental? I think not. I needed the floodgates of heaven to pour out, so I made the commitment to tithe from that day forward, and I've never looked back.

Right after my son turned four is when his dad moved out for the last time. He had come to live with us for about six months in our last and final attempt to save our marriage. My son was so excited to have all of us back under the same roof. That afternoon was like a Lifetime movie unfolding before my eyes. As his dad was packing his bags, my son was pleading through his tears, "Why are you leaving, Daddy?! You were supposed to be with us forever!" He kept saying that over and over as he clung to his bags so they couldn't be zipped. All I could do was hold him tight so he wouldn't chase after his daddy. We sat there in the middle of my bedroom floor intertwined like a pretzel sobbing for what seemed like hours.

The weeks following, my son was very angry. I was so worried that my little boy would be scarred for life, so I was determined to do whatever

I had to do to make sure that didn't happen. I met with a counselor at church who suggested we needed to redirect his emotions into something positive. I prayed for the financial means to be able to send him to Cathedral Academy, our church's school, and I truly believe it was the act of tithing I had started the year prior that made it possible. The numbers on paper didn't make sense, as it was a hefty monthly payment, but I committed to God that as long as He would provide, I would send my son there.

He began K4 there that fall, and it was the best decision I could've made. His anger slowly but surely started to soften as he had life and Scripture pouring into him. We kept him busy so he didn't focus on his pain, and even though we'd have many nights of, "When are you and Daddy getting back together?" we kept pressing forward. I'd just reassure him that God is in control, and He would work everything out for good.

He started 6th grade there this year. It is has been extremely important for him to see how God has provided. While I've never disclosed the painful details of the divorce to him, I've always let him see me cry, ask for forgiveness when I let my anger get the best of me, talk through how to handle certain situations and which Scriptures helped me through. I thought it was a good learning experience for him to see that I wasn't perfect, and I needed to depend on God for everything. If I didn't know what to do, we pulled out our Bible to see what God suggested, and we prayed like crazy.

I pray that he always remembers that. When he's older and faced with tough situations, I hope he pulls out his Bible and looks to the only One who can truly help us at the deepest level when we're hurting or needing direction. I passed onto him what I had learned that tithing is an act of worship to give back to God what is rightfully His. He has seen the Lord bless over us financially and so he knows this to be true. I don't think there's any greater blessing then when we can show our kids that God is faithful to keep His Word because that truth creates a foundation for their faith that they can hold onto forever.

. . . .

Not only will God provide financially, but He is also the source of joy, peace, comfort, and all of the wonderful things in life.

"God is the source of life through His provision. The enemy is the source of lies through his perversion." (TerKeurst 2017)

In the Finding I Am study, Lysa explains the seven I AM statements of Jesus. The first one covered is, *"I am the bread of life." – John 6:35, NIV.* She explains the difference between *bios,* or physical life, and *zoe,* the fullness of life. We are not just called to live but to live life to the fullest.

Jesus says, *"The thief comes only to steal and kill and destroy; I have come that they may have life and have it to the full."*
– JOHN 10:10, NIV

So many of us go through life day by day doing the same thing over and over until life loses its meaning and becomes more of a routine than anything we enjoy. When life loses its meaning, we become dead inside. Our eyes may be open and we may be breathing, but the light is not on. In our younger days, we may have looked for something more. A dream to follow. But how many times were we set back? How many times were we told to wake up and become a part of the "real world?" But really, when we lose our craving for something more, we shut down. We become complacent.

The company I worked for before I started working from home had a safety motto, "Complacency kills." The purpose was to remind people to open their eyes to the moment at hand and be present. How many of us have gotten in our cars to drive home and then can't remember how we got there once we were safe in our driveway? Not only can complacency kill us physically if we're not careful but also mentally and emotionally. If we lose sight of our purpose, we shift into autopilot and become zombies.

I've never watched the show "The Walking Dead" because I don't like zombies, but the title sounds so fitting to our society today.

I cannot count the times I have heard people say, "I just want to go into work, put in my time, and then go home." *Put in my time* sounds like a prison to me. That's not to say that every office job can't be rewarding, but it's all about your mindset. If your job inspires you and is meaningful, that is awesome! If you lose a little bit of your soul every day you don't feel like you're making a difference, then it might be time for a change.

Some of us might be in a place where we can't change where we work at the moment. Good jobs can be hard to come by. If that is you, don't lose hope. You need to find a way to get re-inspired. To spark whatever it is inside of you that makes you feel alive.

We all have God-given gifts that help us fulfill our purpose. Maybe yours is the ability to sing. Even if you can't audition for America's Got Talent to win a million dollars or become famous overnight, how can you use that gift right where you are? Maybe you can join your church's worship team. Or go to your local nursing home and brighten their day with your entertainment.

I will never forget when I visited my grandmother and a local orchestra came to play at her nursing home. They were playing songs that were popular in the residences' day, and as I looked around the room, I could see the light switch come on in so many of their eyes. The music took them back to a time when they felt inspired. It sparked memories that put smiles on their faces and a little rhythm in their soul. Even if only for a moment, I saw my grandmother come alive again.

We all have our own "circle of influence." People that are put in our lives for a reason. Either for us to help, or for them to help us. Have you noticed them lately? Do you know why they're there? We don't have to be well-known to make a difference. A smile to a stranger could have more of an impact then you will ever know. But we don't have to understand the impact. In fact, many times, we will never know the difference we made in someone's life, but I can tell you that if you live in a way that gives life and hope to others, you *will* make a difference.

There's an awesome local event in Moncks Corner, SC, that I went to called "Bloom." A group of women came together to share their gifts in a variety of ways. Some had craft tables set up while others were selling products that were meaningful to them. Those that were gifted with public speaking stood up and offered their testimonies to inspire and teach.

The saying "Bloom where you're planted" was the theme. It means using our gifts to influence those in our circle to prove that average day to day women can have an impact right from their own living room in their jammies chasing after a toddler. For more information on the event, you can check out the website *http://kerilynnsnyder.com/bloom*.

We all want to live a life of significance. But some of us are so broken that we can't see ourselves as important. First, you have to correct your thinking and realize there is still beauty in the broken. Your purpose isn't so much about what you do but about *who you are*. When I turned thirty, that's when I really started digging deep into who I was. What I liked and disliked. What I valued and desired. What truly spoke to my heart. When I discovered who I was, then I could better define my purpose.

I love rocking babies. And so, I serve in my church nursery. But I can't make a living off of rocking babies. When I dug deeper, I found that the root of why I love snuggling a baby is because I love helping someone in need. Babies are dependent. They are vulnerable. They need love to grow and flourish. I can do that. I thrive when I feel needed. My gifts of mercy and service involve taking care of others.

Well, I've worked in the aluminum industry for the past thirteen years. From the surface, it doesn't seem like the ideal place to use my gifts. But in reality, customers are still people who struggle with life issues. Connect with them on a personal level, and you will build relationships that will grow deep roots. People who feel nurtured will remember you. It's been said that most people won't remember what you've said to them, but they will remember how you made them feel. If you journey with a customer through life struggles, then their loyalty goes beyond business.

So, once I realized how I could use my natural gifts within my circle of influence, then I could feel like my life was more than just a job where

I spent the majority of my day. If I was going to be away from my child, I needed my work to mean something. You've probably heard the saying "It is what it is." But what I've learned is more like, "It is what you make it." You can find joy and abundant life when you tap into what you've already been given – your gifts, the people around you and making the most of what you have.

A few months after my son and I moved out, I joined a Bible study on Esther by Beth Moore. Great study! The inspiration from that was "you were designed for such a time as this." You are where you are for a reason. You have the gifts you've been given for a reason. Maybe life doesn't look like how you wanted it to, me too. But that phrase has been the driving force behind living in the present for "such a time as this" and using what I have to get me to the next season.

God will meet you where you are. And He will be faithful to complete the good work that He started in you. Even if you took a few detours. Don't settle for a life of complacency. Don't let what Jesus did on the cross to set you free not have meaning. Live in the moment rather than let the moments pass you by.

"And I am certain that God, who began the good work within you, will continue his work until it is finally finished on the day when Christ Jesus returns."

– Philippians 1:6, NLT

Paul is declaring this from inside his jail cell. He was physically in shackles yet still hopeful. I don't think he could have said this with confidence unless He knew God's heart. To know *of* God is different than to *know* God. My prayer is that those of us feeling imprisoned within our own minds can let Paul's certainty become a key to unlock the chains we let the enemy use to drag us down until we feel paralyzed. Take back your life. And live each day to the fullest.

. . . .

Another aspect of God's provision that is important to note is that it requires our *patience.*

"Faith in God includes faith in His timing." - Neal A. Maxwell

Let's be honest here, waiting is not always easy nor is it fun. It is usually bearable if you know how long you have to wait. But not knowing if you will ever get your heart's desires on this side of heaven can be daunting.

Thankfully there are verses you can cling to if you're waiting on something. Here are just a few.

"But those who wait for the LORD shall renew their strength; they shall mount up with wings like eagles; they shall run and not be weary; they shall walk and not faint."

– ISAIAH 40:31, NKJV

"The LORD is good to those who wait for him, to the soul who seeks him."

– LAMENTATIONS 3:25, NKJV

"Therefore, I will look to the Lord; I will wait for the God of my salvation; my God will hear me."

– MICAH 7:7, NKJV

"Blessed is the man who remains steadfast under trial, for when he has stood the test he will receive the crown of life, which God has promised to those who love him."

– JAMES 1:12, ESV

"Therefore do not worry, saying, 'What shall we eat?' or 'What shall we drink?' or 'What shall we wear?' For after all these things the Gentiles seek. For your heavenly Father knows that you need all

these things. But seek first the kingdom of God and His righteous-
ness, and all these things shall be added to you."
— MATTHEW 6: 31-33, NKJV

It is comforting for me to know that all I have to do is seek God and He will provide. His timing is not always what I would choose, however, I wait, and I will trust because He has proven to me over and over that His timing is perfect. At least on a weekly basis, if not daily, I am reminded of this truth.

Just this week for example, I overcommitted and had an extremely tight schedule. I had decided that I would just make the best of it and do what I had to do to get everything done. But then, God worked it out. Things fell off my to-do list naturally, and I ended up getting everything caught up that I needed to. And by naturally, I literally mean, a snow storm came through Charleston and basically closed the city for days. I didn't have to cancel anything, it just happened to work out.

Now, I'm not saying that God made it snow because I needed help with a busy schedule. What I am saying is that I believe when I submit my schedule to the Lord and put forth my best effort, then he blesses that decision and works everything out for good.

When I began house hunting, immediately I found one that I loved. It seemed to be the perfect fit, but the owner didn't accept my offer. I found a second house that was the same layout as the first, but I didn't love it as much. I still made an offer but didn't get it. But then, a third house came on the market just right around the corner from the other two. It was perfect! Better price. Better layout. Better location. And I have wonderful neighbors!

Ever since I made the decision to walk with the Lord, things just seem to flow a little more easily. I'm no longer in a constant battle for control. I don't try to force things to happen. Because if I do, it never seems to work out. If I would have paid the asking price for the first house just to have what I thought I wanted, I would never have known the blessings I have in this house.

While I am still waiting on the biggest desire of my heart, I am thankful for the reminders that God's timing will be just what we need.

. . . .

Other verses:

"And this same God who takes care of me will supply all your needs from his glorious riches, which have been given to us in Christ Jesus."
— PHILIPPIANS 4:19, NLT

"Ask, and it will be given to you; seek, and you will find; knock and the door will be opened to you."
— MATTHEW 7:7, NIV

"And whatever you ask in prayer, you will receive, if you have faith."
— MATTHEW 21:22, ESV

♪ *Song: "Good, Good Father" by Chris Tomlin*

Small Group – Session 2

Provision

1. God doesn't just provide financially. Where do you need God to provide for you in your life?
2. Is there any area that you might be overstretching your budget? What adjustments could you make?
3. Do you find it hard to give 10% of your gross income? If you already are committed to this, how has it blessed/changed your life?
4. Do you feel "stuck" in any area of your life? Did the chapter help offer an idea of how you could get re-inspired?
5. What makes you feel alive? Do you incorporate that into your daily routine?
6. Have you identified your circle of influence (coworkers, family, friends, neighbors)? How can you use your gifts to make a difference in their lives? If you don't know your gifts, take the free test at www.giftstest.com.
7. Do you feel like you're living out your purpose? If not, how can you still use your gifts where you are?

ACCEPTANCE

. . .

E arly on in my journey, there was a church service around Easter where little cards were attached to a cross at the front of the stage. Each card had a word on it. There was an alter call for the congregation to come up and grab a card from the cross. My word was "Acceptance." I didn't know how that applied to me at the time, but I soon would find out.

That spring, I joined a small group at church called Divorcecare. We went through the different stages of grief and healing, and one of the steps was Acceptance. In addition to the class, I would receive daily devotional emails that would talk about acceptance. The church services also seemed to carry the same message. When God is trying to talk to us, He usually does so through multiple channels. He knows I need the repetition so I can fully get what He's trying to say.

There were many things that I realized I needed to accept. If you don't accept it, you can't move past it. So, we were tasked to sit down and make a list of everything we were losing with the divorce. I needed healing, but I needed to fully understand what I needed healing from. It would take a couple years until I understood the depth of the loss, but the Lord was always so patient with me as I processed each hurt. The cycle of anger would often start back over when I realized something new, so I also had to be patient with myself.

So, let's talk about a few things…

Lifestyle – Since I wasn't married ten years, I couldn't get alimony. It's not like he had much to offer anyway in regard to finances. I actually had begun to get into a healthier situation with my finances on my own. I didn't own a credit card until recently. But it was the little things like trading in my SUV, not having cable, not being able to take vacations, etc. There were many lifestyle changes that I had to accept being on a single income.

Probably the biggest hurdle for my emotions was feeling rejected. We slowly started not being invited to certain get togethers because the crowd mainly consisted of married couples and their children. Their families were growing with each little baby they welcomed, and well for us, it was just my son and me. I wasn't sure if they felt sorry for us or uncomfortable. I finally came to a place where I could understand, but it took me a while to accept it.

Companionship – Even though I am very much introverted, I love having people to do life with. I have grown to be ok with doing things on my own, but it's always so much nicer when you have someone to share it with. I have my son, of course, for which I am so thankful, but I can't talk to him like I can an adult. I get especially chatty at night after he's asleep. I enjoy processing my day after I crawl into bed at night. Some of my friends stay up late, so I can chat with them, but most of the time it's just me.

The Lord has really drawn near to me in those moments of my loneliness. The Bible says, *"Draw near to God, and He will draw near to you."* – *James 4:8, ESV.* Every time I have ever tested Scripture, all I have found is truth. I so enjoy watching the Lord work in my life and the fact that He loves me enough to show me that He is still very much alive and present in our day to day lives. He is the God of the entire universe, yet He takes time to spend with me. That blows my mind!

When I began my journey, I didn't really believe that God would want to spend time with me. In my mind, He was always an authority figure with a status much too important for little ole me. Why would He want to listen to me ramble about my problems? And I never understood how people actually talked to God. Did they really hear Him? I didn't.

I read a lot of Priscila Shirer's books. Two of my favorites were *Discerning the Voice of* God and *He Speaks to Me*. As I spent time with the Lord and have grown to know Him, I have learned to hear His whispers. I personally have never heard the audible voice of God, although I do know some who have. For me, it's more of a thought that comes into my mind.

"Whether you turn to the right or to the left, your ears will hear a voice behind you, saying, 'This is the way; walk in it.'"
— ISAIAH 30:21, NIV

If it aligns with God's Word, then I believe it is from Him. If it contradicts His Word in anyway or makes me feel guilt, shame, or things from the enemy, then I know that thought has to go. I try to be intentional to take each thought captive and only keep the ones that are life giving.

"We demolish arguments and every pretension that sets itself up against the knowledge of God, and we take captive every thought to make it obedient to Christ."
— 2 CORINTHIANS 10:5, NIV

Our pastor recently did a whole series about Breakthrough and how the battlefield is in our mind. He said, "Whatever thought you don't take captive will take you captive." The voice we are listening to will determine the direction we go. Thoughts become actions so we must direct them down the path that will bring life rather than death. When we submit our thoughts under God's truth, then we release His power in our lives.

In order to hear God's voice, we must become familiar with His voice. And we do that by reading His Word. This is true of any foreign language. If you hear someone speaking in Italian for the first time, you probably won't have any idea what they are saying. But as you lean in and listen, or even get CD's from the library and learn the language, then you will be able to identify more and more words. The more you immerse yourself in the new language, the quicker you will be able to recognize what you are hearing.

You also must know what the Word says in order to know what thoughts to cast out. Otherwise, the enemy can put a thought in your mind that you receive and then he just steps back while you take over and bully yourself. "My husband cheated on me because I wasn't good enough." If I don't counteract that lie with what God says, then it's easy to let it become what I think about myself.

> "For as he thinks in his heart, so is he."
>
> – PROVERBS 23:7, NKJV

We become what we think about. So, I choose to think about verses like this when I need encouragement. God says I'm wonderful and so I am.

> "For you created my inmost being; you knit me together in my mother's womb. I praise you because I am fearfully and wonderfully made."
>
> – PSALM 139: 13-14, NIV

And He has good plans for me even when things go wrong. Detours happen. But my future is hopeful.

> "For I know the plans that I have for you, declares the LORD, plans to prosper you and not to harm you, plans to give you hope and a future."
>
> – JEREMIAH 29:11, NIV

An assistant pastor at our church gave a message about this on New Year's Eve. He said, "Our thoughts can either crown us or cripple us." It's a choice. I want to be prosperous and successful, so I need to keep the Word in my mind and on my lips day and night. I need to know the truth, so I don't get distracted by the lies.

"Keep this Book of the Law always on your lips; meditate on it day and night, so that you may be careful to do everything written in it. Then you will be prosperous and successful."

– JOSHUA 1:8, NIV

"But you are a chosen generation, a royal priesthood, a holy nation, His own special people, that you may proclaim the praises of Him who called you out of darkness into His marvelous light."

– 1 PETER 2:9, NKJV

Intimacy - I miss having someone to hold me and tell me everything is going to be alright after a hard day or that certain week of the month when I am feeling especially pessimistic (if you haven't read Stasi Eldridge's book *Becoming Myself*, you definitely should! Page 50 explains the emotional rollercoaster of hormones that every woman can relate to.)

One of my main love languages is physical touch. While hugs from friends and snuggles from my son and our puppy definitely fill my love tank, let's be honest – after being married and sleeping with a man for years, there are certain desires that are hard to live without when you know what you're missing! I'm not quite sure I've accepted this one, but until I find the husband God has for me, I'm considering this my cross to bear. To some who don't share the love language of physical touch, this may seem trivial, but sometimes, it seems unbearable.

Years keep passing by, and I see gravity taking its toll on my body. Since I've turned thirty, I've felt like I'm in the prime of my life with no one to share it with. So many nights I've regretted all of the times I said, "No, I'm too tired." I try to encourage my married friends to take advantage of every opportunity because you never know when it might be your last.

Just like that, things can change, and you don't fully appreciate what you had until it's no longer yours. We so often rush through life in survival mode that we miss salvaging the sweetness of every "last" moment in our lives – the last time you give your child a bath, the last time you carry them to bed or sing them lullabies. I wonder how much longer we would linger in the moment if we knew it would be our last.

Precious Moments – Above all, the biggest sacrifice is the moments I miss when my son is with his dad. Even though I try to use the time he's not with me wisely so that I get all of my errands done and can just enjoy him when he's home, it doesn't change the fact that I still miss out on time that I can never get back.

Our kids grow up so fast! When you're in the thick of it, the younger years and sleepless nights seem to last forever, but the truth is that the days may seem long, but the years are short. Before you know it, your babies are all grown up. They don't need you to rinse the soap out of their hair or their sandwiches cut in fours. The little things you once felt so unappreciated for doing now become precious memories you reminisce over.

When I think of birthday parties I miss and Christmas celebrations, I can find myself getting a little bitter. I try to think he's lucky that he gets to experience two of everything, but if I'm being honest, I still hurt for him. Nothing hurts my heart more than to see his heart ache because he misses his dad. Each of us provides something for him that the other doesn't, and it's not fair that he can't have both of us under the same roof. Thankfully he can pick up the phone and Facetime us whenever he needs us, but I can't help but think of the moments when he needs his Mommy's snuggles to tell him everything will be ok and I'm not there. The only thing that helps me is knowing that he knows how to draw near to God in those moments he needs comfort.

. . . .

I had a revelation the other morning as I called my son to the table for breakfast. A big part of how we perceive our life is based on how we label things, so in other words – it's all in what you call it. For example, my sweet little neighbor often invites me over to have coffee with her in her "breakfast room." The ring of that sounds so inviting, "Come join me in my breakfast room." So, as I put our breakfast on the table the other morning, I started to call out, "Come to the table," and then my mind shifted and I heard myself say, "Your eggs are ready. Please come to the breakfast room."

I pondered why changing what I called it made such a big difference in how I felt about it. I thought about my neighbor's breakfast room. It really isn't anything special. It is your typical dine-in kitchen. When I think of a breakfast room, I picture a cozy, grandeur room in more of an elegant setting. I'm not sure why, as really the words literally mean a room where you eat breakfast. And then I started thinking about how other labels we put on things in our life affect our outlook.

We can wake up each morning and say to ourselves, "I hate that I HAVE to go to work today." Or we can wake up and think, "I am so grateful that I have a job and I GET to provide for my family." We can think of things either as a burden or a privilege. Either way, most of us will get up and go to work regardless, but who do you think will have a better day – the person with the negative outlook or positive outlook?

We also can have a tendency to be judgmental of others. When we go into their homes and see a mess, we often think they are just not clean people. Sometimes true, but the flip side could be:

Dirty dishes mean I feed my family.
Full trash can means I clean up after them.
Messy floors mean I let my children have fun.
Pile of unfolded laundry means I keep my
family in clean clothes.
Wet bathroom means my kid took a shower!

This reminds me of something else I saw on Facebook that really changed my perspective.

To the pregnant women on social media posting constant updates and belly pictures... I love seeing how excited you are to become a mommy.

To the women posting "selfies"... thanks for letting young girls know that it's okay to love yourself and to feel beautiful!

To the mom posting a million pictures of her kids... it makes my heart so happy to see parents so proud of and loving their babies!

To the married couple constantly posting "sappy love posts"... thank you for being a reminder to the next generation that all hope isn't lost and happy marriages most definitely DO exist.

To the business owners who constantly post about their businesses... keep going! Your strong will and passion for what you do is astounding! Even in the midst of all the negative remarks, you keep on going for yourself and your family!

To the person posting about their fitness journey & how they decided to change their lifestyle for health reasons or just to look or feel better about themselves... I love seeing your progress pictures, your healthy meals, your gym check-ins. I especially love seeing your before and after pictures!!

To the stay at home mom always bragging & posting about how awesome their days go being able to cook and or bake often for their family... I love seeing all you can do with your kids & all those pictures you get to take of the moments you don't want to forget.

To the mom posting about how challenging their days can be because she has a job either because she needs to or simply because she loves her career.... I love seeing how you manage yourself to be a good mom, good wife & a hard working mom.

Let's stop being annoyed by everything and start lifting each other up!!! (Maner 2016)

Instead of rolling your eyes next time you see something that annoys you on social media, try looking at it from a different perspective.

Another example is thinking, "I have to feed the kids," rather than, "I am blessed with kids to feed." Do we see our kids as a burden or a gift? An opportunity to love and be loved? A chance to leave an imprint on this world and hopefully make a positive impact? Or just something else on our never ending to do list?

When I was in the midst of my struggling and feeling very depressed about the divorce, I was very hard on myself as a mother. Nothing I did ever felt good enough. At the end of my fourteen - fifteen-hour day, once he was finally asleep for the night, I'd collapse on the couch and wonder if I had been successful that day. I fed him – but did he have a well-rounded diet? How many fruits/veggie servings? ...He had clean clothes – but where his pants high-waters because he was growing taller before my very eyes? Was he warm enough without a jacket? Did I teach him anything? Did I make the most of every moment? What could I have done differently?

The Mommy guilt was never-ending. I wished I had been more intentional with persuasive tactics instead of screaming and nagging. I longed to have more hours in the day to do fun crafts and stimulate his creative side instead of turning on the TV to get a little peace and quiet and let my mind wind down from work.

And then there was work! Certain times of the month required longer hours. I was bringing work home and while I tried to work after he was asleep, some days I knew I wouldn't have the energy to stay awake. The demands for my time seemed overwhelming and many days it didn't seem like I had accomplished anything. And then I decided something... even if I wasn't supermom that day, if at bare minimum the only thing I did was to give him a hug and kiss and tell him I love him...then that was a successful day!

I had to accept that parenting was different now that it was just me. I couldn't compare myself to the moms who had a partner to share the workload of running a household or the resources of two incomes. I had to make the best of our circumstances and change my perspective from everything I HAD to do to everything I GOT the opportunity to enjoy.

How much time do we spend hating our current situation? But how much would we appreciate it if things were worse? I wonder how things in our lives might change for the better if we changed the way we think. I'm not saying call things what they're not. That would be lying to yourself. But I do think that sometimes faking it until you make it works.

That's kind of how living with expectant faith works. You have a dream in your heart. You're not quite where you thought you'd be, but you keep trusting God and taking steps toward where He's leading you. All the while, you're keeping a positive attitude with your end destination in mind.

So, while it's important to make the list of things you are losing in the divorce/break-up so that you can accept them and move on, you then need to reevaluate your perspective on the overall situation. Meaning at the end of the day, you can either think, "Look at all I've lost. I'm the victim here." Or you can choose to believe, "This may hurt for now, but I will be stronger because of it. And thank you God for new beginnings. I get to start over. I'm not stuck in an unhappy marriage for the rest of my life. Not everyone gets a second chance."

Ultimately, it's your decision. In every situation, you can either become *bitter* or *better*. Just like a coin, there's always two sides. I'd much rather come out "a*head*" than a tail!

. . . .

Something else to consider:

The same boiling water that softens the potato hardens the egg. It's about what you're made of, not the circumstances.

The number one thing the Lord looks for is a willing heart. We don't have to be perfect or have it all together. But if our heart is humbled enough to let God come in and mold us into who He created us to be so we can rise above our circumstances, then He will be faithful to do so. If you need a little inspiration, search "Andra Day's *Rise Up.*" That song ignites a fire inside of me to do better. Because let's face it, every day we will mess up and fall short, even if it's something as simple as raising your voice when you set a goal not to. But it doesn't mean we have to stay stuck in our regrets. We can make the choice to rise up and do better the next day.

Accepting your life and settling are two very different things. In order to progress, you have to first accept the past. You might stay in this season for a little while and that's ok. This is where you grieve, you work through your anger, you forgive, and then you get to a point where you want something better. You make the choice to live in the present with your desired end game in mind.

Settling is when you decide that this is all your life is going to be and that's it. You're in survival mode, the most basic way to live. Joyful moments are few and far between. You may not even remember the last time you were truly happy. You doubt that you are worthy of anything better. When you don't know what to do, it's easy to do nothing.

But doing nothing is also a decision for things to stay the way they are. No, you can't change that your husband has given up or that your child refuses to respect you. But you can decide how you will make the necessary changes for YOU to get out of this rut.

Think for a moment how life would be if our toddler never graduated potty training. It can be tough. Hard to understand why they can't continue life as they know it. The change may not make sense to them. But we urge them as parents that in order to get to the next season of their life, they must trust us. Fighting it will only prolong the inevitable. There is a whole other world of "big girl/boy" panties awaiting them if they can just push through. Can you imagine their life if they didn't? If they settled on the fact that sitting in their own mess was good enough.

If I were to ask you right now, "Are you excited about your life?" would the answer be yes or no? If yes, that's awesome! Keep that passion burning inside of you! You will do great things!

If the answer is no, find out what inspires you and then go after it. When you are filled up, you will be amazed at how much easier the relationships around you seem. We cannot place the expectation on others to fill us up and do what only God can do. He knows us better than we know ourselves. He is the source of abundant life.

Take a moment to digest the Scripture below.

"For since their rejection meant that God offered salvation to the rest of the world, their acceptance will be even more wonderful. It will be life for those who were dead!"

– ROMANS 11:15, NLT

I almost skimmed right past this gem, and then I paused. My rejection was my divorce. It was the most painful season of my life. One I wasn't sure I would ever get through. But I accepted it, and I chose to not let that be the end of my story.

And now I can share with each of you my journey of how God saved me from becoming the bitter, mean woman I once felt justified to be. If even one of you decides that you too want to know Jesus because you've heard my story, then that makes my pain even more wonderful because you chose life!

. . . .

Other verses:

"And I want you to know, my dear brothers and sisters, that everything that has happened to me here has helped to spread the Good News."

– PHILIPPIANS 1:12, NLT

"As for us, we cannot help speaking about what we have seen and heard."

– ACTS 4:20, NIV

♪ *Song: "Unfinished" by Mandisa*

Small Group – Session 3

Acceptance

1. Have you heard/seen a repetitive message/theme that keeps popping up in your life? What might God be trying to speak to you through that?
2. Would you say that you have fully processed your hurt? Could there be anything you hadn't thought of that you need to spend time revisiting to ensure you can be fully healed?
3. Do you take time throughout the day to stop and hear what God might be whispering to you?
4. Are your thoughts about yourself crowning or crippling you? Is there any "stinking thinking" you need to take captive? Choose a Scripture you could replace the lie with.
5. Reminisce over a fond "last" memory.
6. Do you have an area of your life where you need a perspective shift? How could this change your current situation?
7. Is there any area where you feel you are settling?

RELEASE

...

A fter I accepted the things I couldn't change, I had to let it go. I had to forgive and release. My sweet friend who walked with me during the divorce sent me a card that said, "Stop looking back, you're not going that way." Meaning the past is the past, and it's not meant to be brought into our future.

> *"Beloved, I do not consider that I have made it my own; but this one thing I do: forgetting what lies behind and straining forward to what lies ahead."*
> — PHILIPPIANS 3:13, NRSV

Painful moments are horrible enough going through once. Then why do we torture ourselves by reliving them in our minds over and over? Thinking about it isn't going to change what happened or what was said. Staying there only creates a bigger hole inside of us that takes longer to dig back out of. Sometimes it feels safe in our holes, but that's just a lie the enemy tells us to trick us into isolation. That is why it is so critical that we have a group of people around us that can speak life into those situations that seem dark and overwhelming.

I just saw the movie The Shack. Talk about extreme cases of forgiveness – wow! I can't even imagine having to forgive someone for taking the life of my child, nor do I ever want to. Each of us has hurts in our lives that need the healing of forgiveness in order to move past the situation. Whatever we are not healed from, we inflict on others. You may have heard the saying, "Hurt people, hurt people." That is so true! We see it all the time. The vicious circle of abuse and addiction in families can go on for generations. It takes a strong person to be able to forgive and then change the pattern.

If you haven't seen the movie, I highly recommend it! It really brings to life what harboring unforgiveness and hurt does to our bodies. Not to mention, it makes us numb to be able to see other's pain around us. We don't forgive others for them; we forgive them for our own healing and then we release them to God.

A couple of years after the divorce, I thought I was completely healed and moved on. Until one Sunday, our pastor said, "You know you've truly forgiven someone when you can pray for them." Whoa! Wait – I could say I forgave my ex and his girlfriend. I could even say I was no longer mad about everything. But pray for them?? That had not crossed my mind. I mean sure, I prayed that she would be a good stepmom to my son and that they would be good role models for him, but everything was for my son's sake, not theirs.

I had never actually spoken their names out loud in my prayers. And to be honest, the first time I tried, my tongue felt like a ton of bricks physically restricting me from being able to do so. It was one of the weirdest feelings, but as I pushed through, it became easier and easier.

My pastor suggested journeying through Psalms and letting the prayers of David comfort me as I too struggled to forgive "my enemies." I knew I was called to love my enemies, but when I had to put love into action and really mean what I was praying for them (all good things of course), then it became real. This was a whole different level of forgiveness that I wasn't even aware of, but again the Lord is so patient to give us what we can handle.

So, I released both of them from any unforgiveness just as I had to release my son into God's care when I can't be there to protect him.

There's something about *speaking* the release that makes it become alive. Would God care for my son when I couldn't? Absolutely! But speaking it is what settled the worry in my heart that I didn't have control over his safety when he wasn't with me. It activated the promise of God's covering and protection.

Not only did I need to forgive them, but I also needed to seek forgiveness from God. I had said some pretty nasty things to both of them throughout the affair. Regardless of their choices, I had my own part to play. But thank goodness for this –

"If we confess our sins, he is faithful and just to forgive us our sins, and to cleanse us from all unrighteousness."
– 1 JOHN 1:9, NKJV

And I know this to be true for a couple of reasons. As I read back through the journals I kept through all of this, I found an entry where I actually prayed for their marriage. If you had asked me years ago if I ever imagined wishing the two people who had put me through hell and back well in their new life together, I would have looked at you sideways. And maybe had a few choice words too.

But at some point, something shifted, and the bitterness melted away. I honestly meant what I prayed, and I had no intention of ever telling another soul. My heartfelt prayer was between the Lord and I. But I tell you now because I celebrate how far God has brought me in my journey. And if my heart can be changed, then so can yours. The release is a choice. You won't be disappointed by what's on the other side!

And one day, you may even find yourself texting with your archrival about your kid's school pictures and even smile a little. And then you'll stand in awe of how good forgiveness feels, and your heart will swell with gratitude towards the one who heard your prayer,

"Create in me a clean heart, O God, and renew a steadfast spirit within me."

– PSALMS 51:10, NKJV

And He will answer, *"I will give you a new heart and put a new spirit in you."* – *Ezekiel 36:26, NLT* and *"This means that anyone who belongs to Christ has become a new person. The old life is gone; a new life has begun!*

– 2 CORINTHIANS 5:17, NLT

. . . .

So not only do we need to release the people in our life who have hurt us, but we also need to release our faith. We do this not only by our actions, taking steps in faith, but also speaking it. No - *declaring* it. Spoken words are powerful. They release things into the air and have the power to set things in motion. When we build others up with our words and encourage them, that sets them on course to be confident, successful and fruitful. But when we tear them down with our words, that can change their whole outlook on life and what they will be able to accomplish.

It's the same thing when we make an agreement with God. When we declare what we are believing for by speaking it, we invite Him into our situations. Once we invite Him, anything is possible.

One of my dear friends shared her story on tithing in service one Sunday. She grew up in church so she was familiar with how tithing worked, and she didn't doubt that it did. But there came a time in her life where finances were tight, so she made the decision to stop tithing for a season. Then our pastor spoke about the importance of giving back to God and how if we honor Him in that, He will rebuke the devourer for our sake.

She knew the promise. The promise was always there. It never changed. But her faith had waivered, and once she realized she needed to bring her faith up to the promise, that allowed God to step in and act on her behalf. And He did. Because He always does.

God loves to step in and redeem a bad situation. He is a good, good father at the very core of His being. But we have to believe that and give Him permission to come into our lives. We have to surrender every area to Him. Once He is granted access, He can work all things together for good. He didn't create us to be slaves submitting to His every demand. He won't barge in, even though He has the power to do so. God is a gentleman.

. . . .

"God! She cried out; change is so hard! She heard his reply deep in her heart. What if change is actually just me unveiling who you really are?" (Eldredge 2013)

Another thing we have to release into God's hands is the process. Mending a broken heart is not done overnight. It will feel like you're on a roller coaster ride. Some people find that thrilling, I find it terrifying. This is where my son would insert the story about when we went to Carowinds and they talked me into going on the roller coaster at the entrance of Snoopy Land. He likes to tell everyone that I screamed and squeezed his hand so tight that it hurt. I can't even deny it. I thought it would be a little slower being in the kids' area but that was not so.

Roller coasters shake me to the core. I cannot stand the feeling of dropping. I need to feel grounded. That is hard when your life turns upside down and everything feels out of control. Sometimes, seasons in your life make you want to just keep your eyes closed tightly and wait until it's over.

I went to a training once for work, and we learned a series of exercises that supported the principle that our mind leads our body. We were told to focus on the point in our lower abdomen about an inch below our navel. This is your physiological center of gravity. When you concentrate on this one spot, your mind and body begin working together. It's amazing how this center of gravity creates a stability in your body even when someone applies pressure to your shoulders to push you forward.

Whenever you find yourself in a stressful situation, you should try your best to quiet your mind. Take a few deep breaths and try to find your center. Once you are refocused, you will make better decisions than if you are spinning out of control.

"Do not conform to the pattern of this world but be transformed by the renewing of your mind. Then you will be able to test and approve what God's will is—His good, pleasing and perfect will."
– ROMANS 12:2, NIV

. . . .

Once you've released the things you need to accept, the people you need to forgive, and the process into God's hands, then God can begin redeeming your situation. Back in the Provision section, I mentioned a phrase "there is beauty in the broken." This reminds me of a story. Picture it, Japan in the late 15th century, Kintsugi revolutionizes the perspective on brokenness ... fellow Golden Girls' fans will get this reference. ☺

They began mending broken objects by filling them with gold. They believe when something has suffered damage and has a history that it becomes more beautiful. The imperfections actually add more value than the original.

I learned about this art form on Mother's Day. A sweet and very wise lady in our congregation by the name of Wanda, shared this as part of her testimony and encouragement to all of us who feel like we don't measure up because of things that have happened in our past. We can't change our past. And we can't always fix things back to how they were. But if we trust the process of allowing God to mend our broken places, there is no doubt He will restore our beauty even more than we could imagine.

"For the Lord takes delight in His people; He crowns the humble with victory."

— PSALM 149:4, NIV

"and provide for those who grieve in Zion—to bestow on them a crown of beauty instead of ashes, the oil of joy instead of mourning, and a garment of praise instead of a spirit of despair. They will be called oaks of righteousness, a planting of the LORD for the display of his splendor."

— ISAIAH 61:3, NIV

"But now, this is what the LORD says—
he who created you, Jacob,
he who formed you, Israel:
"Do not fear, for I have redeemed you; I have summoned you by name; you are mine."

— ISAIAH 43:1, NIV

One of the most important things to remember during the redemption process is to keep a posture of repentance. Repentance is not only confessing your sins but then also turning away from them. Whatever happened in your past can be different in your future. We keep this posture by being thankful. A thankful heart is a magnet for God's hand to be on you.

"Give thanks in all circumstances: for this is God's will for you in Christ Jesus."

— 1 THESSALONIANS 5:18, NIV

One definition of *redeem* is to purchase our release from the captivity of sin with a ransom. Jesus was our ransom. We are not only free from death for our sin but also purified from sin's influence as we grow in Christ.

"Who gave himself for us to redeem us from all wickedness and to purify himself a people that are his very own, eager to do what is good."

– *TITUS 2:14, NIV*

Lisa Bevere sums this up perfectly, *"Don't let the enemy use your history to distract you from your destiny."*

. . . .

Other verses:

"Do not be anxious about anything, but in every situation, by prayer and petition, with thanksgiving, present your requests to God."

– *PHILIPPIANS 4:6, NIV*

♪ *Song: "Redeemed" Big Daddy Weave*

Small Group – Session 4

Release

1. Is there anyone you need to release from unforgiveness (yourself included)? As you go through the forgiveness process, journal along the way so you can go back and see how far you've come later.

2. Are you struggling to bring your faith up to God's promise? Take time to search for Scripture that correlates to your area of struggle and then speak truth over your life. Repeat as needed.

3. Do you need God to redeem a situation in your life? Have you given Him access?

4. When you feel your life spinning out of control, how do you refocus (yoga, meditation, prayer)?

5. Take some time to think about how you can turn your heartbreak into something beautiful. Think of what you needed most during that time and then try to fill that need for someone going through the same situation.

6. If possible, try to find the silver lining in your situation. Can you name one reason you could be thankful during this time? Maybe if for nothing else, because of the people who came into your life because of it?

7. Have you let any part of your history (past) distract you from your destiny (future)? What changes could you make to stop that from happening?

KEEP

. . .

A s I type this section, I have Lauren Daigle's "You Alone" playing in the background. My son asked me why I liked it so much, and the only way I could explain it was as if someone was stroking my spirit in reassurance. Like someone stroking your hair to comfort you. It's a lullaby for my soul.

Ever since I went through my divorce, I have been given new eyes to see how much we can hurt so intensely from the trials of life. Sometimes the pain cuts so deep that it feels impossible to pick ourselves up from our pool of tears. The only thing that touched the innermost part of my spirit enough to give me true hope was being in the Lord's Presence.

As I think of the woman whose heart is breaking and she doesn't know the Lord, I weep. The Lord has given me such a soft spot for women who are trying to survive on their own. It's as if I can feel His pain of watching her cry endlessly and not seeing any way out of her misery. He wants so badly to heal those painful parts of her heart, but He can't get to her.

Everyone thinks once you accept Jesus, life is carefree and grand. While His blessings create opportunities that are amazing and wonderful, life still happens. The storms still come. And Jesus never said they wouldn't. He actually said they would.

"When the storms of life come, the wicked are whirled away, but the godly have a lasting foundation."

— PROVERBS 10:25, NLT

We live in a fallen world where we make our own choices. We can't look at bad things that happen and blame God. We also can't look at everything bad that happens and blame ourselves. Sure, accept the role you play in every situation, yes, but also know that there are multiple things working together that you have no control over. Don't take responsibility for anyone else but yourself.

But do know this, *"God causes everything to work together for the good of those who love Him."* — Romans 8:28, NLT. Bad things will happen. But when they do, if you fix your eyes on Jesus and you let Him lead you through them, you will be amazed at how everything works out. And most of the time even better than you could have ever dreamed or imagined.

I could give countless examples of this verse played out in our lives, but the most recent has been such a blessing. I worked for a company for eleven and a half years, and in that time, I had the opportunity to work in many different departments to build my skill sets. It allowed me to be able to provide a lifestyle for my son that I wouldn't have been able to on a teacher's salary, as I had originally planned when I went to college.

In the last couple of years, I had grown unhappy at the long hours I was putting in, mostly due to sitting in almost two hours of traffic daily. It took away time from my son. We were always rushed. I was stressed out which meant I didn't want to take time to plan healthy meals, I often yelled, and the homework battle about put me over the edge. Something needed to change.

I opened a fortune cookie one day that fall that said, "You will soon change careers." I held onto it but honestly didn't have a lot of faith that it would actually happen. But it planted a seed. I thought maybe I would like to become an occupational therapist. I needed something to get me out of the office and allow for a flexible schedule, and my passion is helping others. But I couldn't figure out how I could go to school full-time, work full-time, raise an 8-year-old and get any sleep. I let that thought sit for a couple months.

On New Year's Day, I came across a picture that spoke to my spirit, but I didn't yet know why. Twenty-one days later, I got a phone call from a customer of mine. "How would you like to come work for me and be able to work from home?" …. After a hundred million thoughts flew through my mind in about two seconds, I remembered a picture I had seen where Jesus was kneeling down to a little girl who was holding a small teddy bear in front of her and saying, "But I love it, God." Jesus has his hand extended asking her if she trusted Him. Behind His back was an even larger teddy bear. In order to receive the blessing, she had to take the first step in faith.

But God, I've worked here for over eleven years. This is my family. I love them. I have a great boss. I have benefits with a 401k match. I have customers that I will miss if I leave. But…. I love it God.

That teddy bear behind Jesus's back represents a life now completely free from the ties of Corporate America. I have a 100% flexible schedule to be able to plan my day however is needed to ensure my family comes first. I can go to the gym. I can go to the grocery store when it's not rush hour. I am home when my son gets off school. I can go to all school functions without taking vacation time. I could finally get him the puppy he's always been wanting.

The list goes on…. but the best part is I'm making more money than I was in just my first year. And because I work for a small company, I get a piece of the profit sharing that otherwise I would never see. I get to reap the benefits of my hard work instead of it trickling down. And my boss is *amazing*! When I wasn't even looking, God saw my need for something more. A seed had been planted months in advance and He was working it all out.

Regardless of your situation, I can promise you this with not a doubt in my mind—*everything* is better with Jesus!! His ways are much higher than ours. He has seen our tomorrows and already knows the best path to take. He will never mislead us, leave us or forsake us. So no matter what you are facing today, if you surrender what you have to Jesus, He will make it more than you could ever do on your own. He alone is what we need above all else.

Friends are the best. You can't ever have enough friends. But your friendships have limitations and boundaries, as they should. You can't expect your friends or family members to be your everything. They can use their gifts to be a blessing in your life, but in the middle of night when they are sleeping and you lay there in the dark feeling hopeless, God is there in those precious moments.

So beloved who doesn't yet know Jesus – and not know of Him but truly know Him as a friend – I pray that something will stir in your spirit when you read this. I pray that the next time you are looking down as tears fall from your eyes or around at your circumstances that seem too much for you to bear, know this, you were never meant to carry this on your own. God created us to have a relationship with Him. He wants to walk with us just like He did with Adam and Eve in the garden. If you bring Him your pain, He will turn it into something beautiful. Just like a mosaic made of broken pieces of glass, He will make you whole.

So keep looking ahead with your eyes focused on Jesus and submit your will to Him. Know that your situation is temporary, and things won't be this way forever. Change is inevitable.

. . . .

One of the things that has kept me going is keeping a temporary mindset. That is why I lived in an apartment for five years. I didn't want to set down roots because I wasn't sure what my life would look like in the next year. If someone special came into my life that I decided to marry, then I wanted to be free to move to the next season with ease.

What I began to realize is that a temporary mindset should not mean keeping your life on hold. As my son grew older, I wanted him to have a yard to play in and space to be outdoors. I also wanted him to be able to run around without the downstairs neighbor puncturing holes in their ceiling with their broom. I realized that it was time to look for a house.

The following spring, we moved into our little home. It was so freeing to be able to vacuum at midnight if I wanted to. And to be in the kitchen watching my son playing in the cul-de-sac with friends his age. Now that he's older, I want him to know how to take care of a house rather than calling a maintenance man to fix things. Trust me, having a maintenance man was not something I took for granted, however. There was a season when that was just what I needed. But there came a point where I felt God was calling us to more.

About four years prior to us moving into our house, a sweet friend of mine gave me a coffee cup that said, *"The Lord is my strength and my song. – Exodus 15:2."* I loved that coffee cup, and I used it often. But I never noticed the inscription on the bottom. One day as I was unloading my dishwasher years later, the words caught my attention – "Coventry Daily Blessings."

Before I can finish the story, I must explain why that caught my attention. I just recently heard Steven Furtick preach about the story of Jacob and Esau – Genesis 32-33. The night before Jacob was scheduled to meet with Esau after many years of running for his life for fear Esau would kill him for stealing his birthright, he stopped in a place that wasn't named. He was alone and afraid and in the middle of nowhere. Pastor Furtick had a refrigerator on stage with the magnetic letters *"no where"* as his visual aid.

He went on to tell how Jacob wrestled with an angel of the Lord all night until the angel blessed him. He wouldn't give up. He continued his journey the next day but with a small limp.

The reunion between the brothers turned out to be so much better than Jacob had imagined. We often work up worst case scenarios in our minds and torture ourselves until the story plays out. Jacob had let fear keep him away for so many years but now had been reunited with his brother. On his journey back, Jacob stopped in the same place where he saw the angel and named it. And he said, "Now I am here." So Pastor Furtick slid the "w" over, and the letters now read *now here.*

This is where my story continues… in the middle of my "no where", my friend gave me that cup to encourage me and lift my spirits. I wrestled with the Lord for years trying to change what I couldn't. And years later, I find myself unloading my dishwasher staring at the words "Coventry Daily Blessings" because I am "now here" on Coventry Ct where I have been blessed with a home that the Lord made for my son and I to enjoy in this next season.

"Sometimes you find yourself in the middle of nowhere. And sometimes in the middle of nowhere you find yourself." –Unknown

. . . .

Other verses:

"For the Lord will be at your side and will keep your foot from being snared."

– PROVERBS 3:26, NIV

"If you pay attention to these laws and are careful to follow them, then the Lord your God will keep his covenant of love with you, as he swore to your ancestors."

– DEUTERONOMY 7:12, NIV

♪ Song: "You Alone" by Lauren Daigle

Small Group – Session 5

Keep

1. What reassures and soothes your soul?
2. Have you accepted responsibility for something you can't control (someone else's actions)? If so, how can you reframe the situation to only accept your role in it?
3. Can you look back and reflect on a time where you saw Romans 8:28 play out in your life?
4. How can a temporary mindset be helpful to you?
5. Do you realize the difference between a temporary mindset and putting your life on hold? Is there a part of your life you have on hold that needs to be reawakened?
6. Have you ever struggled with a fear of something in your mind unnecessarily? How did the reality of events compare with the version you had thought up out of fear?
7. Where do you keep your eyes? On your past looking backwards? Looking down focused on current circumstances and feeling stuck? Or looking up with a certainty of hope to guide you?

LOVED

. . .

I remember it like it was yesterday. My 2-year-old son was asleep upstairs, and I was frantically pacing the hallways waiting for my husband to come home. I wanted so badly to leave the house and go find him, but I couldn't. In my state of despair, I knelt on the ground below the picture of Jesus and fell on my face sobbing and crying out to the Lord, "Help me! I can't continue to live this way. I am miserable but I don't know what to do."

I stayed that way for a long time praying and crying very much like the woman in the last scene of the Strength section. At some point, I told God that if I was going to make it through, I needed Him to pick me up and walk this out with me. My world as I knew it was shattered, and mentally and emotionally, I had to be rebuilt from the ground up. As I hope you can tell from my story so far, He did just that. And He's never left my side since.

> *"I would never have learned to walk with God on healthy feet had I never experienced sitting at His table as a cripple. My emotional and spiritual healing has come from approaching God in my handicapped state and believing I was His child and worthy of His love."*
> (Moore 2013)

. . . .

As I begin to write this section, I'm smiling at how God continues to remind me that His timing is perfect. In every way. Even if I'm still single. It is the day before Good Friday–His ultimate sacrifice and NOTHING says love like what He did on the cross for us. What kind of love carries the sin of the whole world when we don't even deserve it? That kind of love is incomprehensible.

If you have kids, you understand that when they are listening and being so sweet, you want to bend over backwards to give them the whole world. But when they are talking back and disobeying…hmmmm, that's a whole different feeling. But God doesn't feel that way about us. He looks at us in our worst moments and thinks, "All I want to do is love them." That's the difference between love in the flesh and God's unconditional love.

When we walk with him daily and abide in His love, He fills us up with His love so we can love others. He reminds us that even if we feel unloved by the people in our lives, He loves us more than we can ever imagine. Even in the midst of our sorrows, we can feel joy.

"Blessed are those who mourn, for they will be comforted."
                                                    – MATTHEW 5:4, NIV

Blessed…I felt far from blessed. I felt rejected when my husband walked out. But looking back, I can see God's hand on my life. I can see how He brought people into my life during the hard times who have become some of the closest friends that I have today. I was surrounded by single moms in my same boat who needed support and comfort just like I did, and so we were there for each other. I began hosting a single mom's Bible study at my apartment, and we journeyed together for a couple of years.

I watched the movie Collateral Beauty on Easter afternoon as I was waiting to get my son back from his dad's. In case you haven't seen it, Howard (Will Smith) loses his daughter and basically loses himself in his grief. He writes letters to "Time", "Death", and "Love", and with the help of his coworkers, the letters get delivered to actors who bring life to these three concepts. Eventually they awaken his spirit and enable him to come to grips with his reality.

While his circumstances didn't change, he learned to accept them and continue living. This can be extremely hard to bear, especially with the loss of a child, but the movie shows the gravity of the situation when you die internally and just give up instead.

> "But it was because the LORD loved you and kept the oath he swore to your ancestors that he brought you out with a mighty hand and redeemed you from the land of slavery, from the power of Pharaoh king of Egypt. Know therefore that the LORD your God is God; he is the faithful God, keeping his covenant of love to a thousand generations of those who love him and keep his commandments."
>
> – DEUTERONOMY 7: 8-9, NIV

For those of us who have been hurt by a loved one, sometimes it is hard to really believe that the kind of faithful love described above even exists. Let alone from God whom we cannot see or touch. How can He fill our deepest needs? The "how" still blows my mind when I stop and think about it or try to explain it. But I do know it is true.

> "For my thoughts are not your thoughts, neither are your ways my ways," declares the LORD. As the heavens are higher than the earth, so are my ways higher than your ways and my thoughts than your thoughts."
>
> – ISAIAH 55: 8-9, NIV

> "Now to him who is able to do immeasurably more than all we ask or imagine, according to his power that is at work within us."
>
> – EPHESIANS 3:20, NIV

There are many misconceptions about who God is. He is not just a "higher power in the universe" or a "puppet master" who desires to control us. The phrase "his power that is at work *within us*" indicates that His plan for us is a collaboration of love. It's a joint effort of doing life together. The greatest love story ever told. *(See the Father's Love Letter in the back of the book.)*

. . . .

Someone that I admire deeply asked me, "If I am blessed with a successful company, a beautiful family and plenty of stuff but I've never prayed, then why am I blessed? Why should I pray?"

It's not that God cannot work without our prayers, but we pray to stay in relationship with Him. As we spend time with Him reading His word and communicating through prayer, He aligns our heart with His to guide us down the best path of life.

There are plenty of people who are smart and successful. Maybe they are wise and gifted with the knowledge they need to rise to the top on their own. Or maybe they had a devoted parent/grandparent praying blessings into their lives and they just haven't discovered the God that made it all possible. Regardless, I do believe there will come a day when they need God because no matter how far up they've made it, there's nothing that can fill the void in each one of us that only God can fill.

When we don't let God fill us up, we often fall into sin traps. We look for short-term fixes to our fleshy desires. But we all know that those only satisfy for a while before we go right back to needing more. If you feel a void deep inside that you have been unable to fill on your own, I encourage you to lean into God and discover all that He has for you.

I love the way Priscilla Shirer put it in her *Unseen* devotional for Prince Warriors:

"But prayer is vital to fighting and winning as a warrior child of God. We can't just treat it like it's something to do when we feel

like it or to mark off a list. Because it's not just words. It's not just something to do – you know, hoping to make God happy with you for checking in. No, prayer is a gift He's given you. It's your opportunity to communicate anytime directly with the One who holds everything in your life together. And not only that, it's a crucial way of staying plugged into God's heart and being vividly aware that you are personally connected to Him." (pg 169)

Back in the Old Testament days before Jesus, only the holy priests could enter the innermost room of the tabernacle – the Holy of Holies. But when Jesus completed His work on the cross, the veil was torn, and we were all granted access to have direct communication with Him. To think of prayer as a gift really shifted my perspective from something I'm supposed to do to something I get to do.

. . . .

"Love isn't what I have the opportunity to get from this world. Love is what I have the opportunity to give." (TerKeurst 2017)

This shifts our focus from ourselves and allows us to prioritize others. It's amazing how well you can distract yourself from your own pity party by helping someone else in need. Then both parties are blessed.

But before we can truly love others, we must also love ourselves. What do we do when we love someone/thing? We take care of it. But then why sometimes do we feel so guilty about taking care of ourselves?

About a year ago, I made the decision to have a monthly massage. I still feel a little guilty about spending the money sometimes, but what a world of difference it makes on my body! It reduces stress. It releases my muscles from being so tight and causing other issues. I hardly ever go to the doctor since I started finding holistic ways to keep myself healthy. Essential oils have played a big part in this as well. Diffusing them in the air has helped with mood swings, stress, skincare and overall wellness.

Some of us focus so much on eating healthy but don't even consider the toxins you expose your body to from your makeup, lotions or cleaners you come into contact with. We often forget the skin is the largest organ in our body and is crucial to our overall health. I have learned so much about the looseness of FDA regulations when I started doing my research, and it's appalling. Thankfully, there are online stores who put their money into quality products rather than advertising or warehousing, so I encourage you to become informed.

Now, I should mention here that there is a difference between loving yourself and vanity. Vanity is defined as excessive pride in one's appearance. Pride is dangerous. Taking care of yourself and putting some effort into looking and feeling good (massages, nails, hair, etc.) are all positive things. Don't feel guilty about spending time on yourself. But be careful that you're not spending too much time on your appearance that it becomes your #1 priority.

. . . .

How we define love comes a lot from our experiences. How we were raised as children and treated in our relationships plays a major role. Thankfully, I had wonderful parents who made me feel loved growing up. I've had different experiences with dating relationships, however. Lack of commitment made me feel not good enough. Infidelity made me think I was missing something. And the list goes on.

I remember one time, my first love and long-term relationship told me that when I wasn't around, he didn't think of me. That was his justification for flirting with the girls he worked with. And the start of heart break for me. Talk about not feeling special.

Besides the events leading up to my divorce, one of the more painful memories I have in my marriage was when I was pregnant. We had gone to an ultrasound appointment and then stopped to grab lunch to go. I don't even remember why we were arguing but things had escalated by the time we got home, and I just remember him throwing my food on the kitchen floor.

In my mind, I couldn't fathom why he would do that when I was carrying his child. That was an all-time low in our marriage, at that point, and made me feel the most unloved that I ever had. It may not sound like a big deal now, but I felt like he slapped me in the face that day. He did exactly what he knew would hurt me, and that contradicted what I thought love was.

I've mentioned "love language" but in case you don't know what that refers to, Gary Chapman wrote about *The Five Love Languages* – touch, quality time, gifts, acts of service and words of affirmation. We all have at least one primary way that we receive love. When you're in a relationship, it's important to identify how you both receive love so that you know how to build each other up. The dangerous part is if they decide to use them against you. You should never withhold an act of love to get revenge.

My ex didn't need as much quality time as I did. And so to "keep me in check so I didn't become too clingy", he would often hold back. He would say, "Whenever I give you an inch, you take a mile." What?! Who says that to someone they love? Quality time is not something you should need to earn. It should come from a place of love and desire. In my mind, you want to spend time with someone you care about. You want to make them feel loved.

Now, I get that there are people who take things to the extreme but that was not the case with us. In the end, it was his way of distancing himself to have time for other things. It's important to recognize your part in the situation and do self-checks regularly to make sure things aren't one-sided. It's also important that you don't own other people's faults.

When I noticed things changing in our relationship, I of course asked a lot of questions to try and figure things out. I knew something wasn't right, but he kept spinning the situation to make me think that I was crazy to think such things. I was always suspicious and felt like I had to be an FBI agent on call 24/7. It was a miserable feeling, but if he wasn't going to tell me the truth, then I had to find it myself.

Always trust your intuition. Things may not be the worst-case scenario you work up in your mind, but if it doesn't feel right, then something is usually not right. Every time I felt a stir in my spirit that something was off, it was. And it doesn't just have to be cheating. Lying can occur for many reasons. But sneaking around behind your spouse's back is not justified for any reason...unless you're planning a sweet surprise for them. ☺

I realize that these stories may not compare to some of yours, but it doesn't change the fact that they were painful. Years of feeling unloved can wear on a person. So when I first went back to church and they talked about how much God loved me, it took me some time to believe it.

. . . .

I didn't read this book yet, but *Without Rival* by Lisa Bevere is on my list of books to read this year. Someone paraphrased what she says that, "God doesn't love each of His children equally, He loves them *uniquely*." That is why we can all sit in a Sunday service and feel like the message was written just for us. He is faithful to give us what we need.

Just like a parent who has more than one child. What works for one won't necessarily work for the other. Countless times you will hear parents of multiples talking about how surprised they are that their children have completely different personalities even being raised in the same home.

It's the same scenario with teachers. Children have different learning styles. Some are auditory learners while others are hands-on. The important thing to note is not to look at what God is doing in other people's lives and measure it against what He's doing in yours. You have needs that maybe they don't and vice versa. He knows what will speak to your heart because He created you. Trust Him to love you how you were designed to receive love and appreciate the uniqueness of what He does for you.

While you're waiting on the big things, notice the little things...

I was Christmas shopping with my friend, and it was getting late, so we decided to head to the checkout. I had just found a basketball shirt that I wanted to get my son, but she was ready to go, and I couldn't find his size. We proceeded to the registers, and oh what to my wondering eyes should appear...the shirt! And in his size!

And just prior to that store, we had grabbed some dinner at a nearby deli. My friend handed the cashier $10 to pay for her portion, but for some reason, the register said $20 so it was telling her I didn't have to pay. A manager came over to fix the issue and I paid with a credit card. She looked down at the receipt and said, "That's weird, it rang up as $0." I called Discover and sure enough, the transaction went through but at no charge, even though she entered the correct amount.

Some might consider both instances coincidences, but not me. I knew that was my Heavenly Father blessing me so sweetly. Even though I don't yet have a husband, I am still very much loved.

When I get discouraged, this passage from Beth Moore's *Whispers of Hope* encourages me to stay the course.

"Are you waiting on God? Are you anxious because an answer is not coming? Remember no one uses timing better than the One who created time. Just because "the right time...has not yet come" doesn't mean you have to waste time. Use every second of the wait to allow the Father to increase your faith and deepen your trust. Stay so close that when He finally says, "now," He'll only have to whisper."

. . . .

Other verses:

"The Lord will fulfill his purpose for me; your steadfast love, O Lord, endures forever. Do not forsake the work of your hands."

– PSALM 138:8, ESV

"Neither height nor depth, nor anything else in all creation, will be able to separate us from the love of God that is in Christ Jesus our Lord."

– ROMANS 8:39, NIV

"Let the beloved of the Lord rest secure in him, for he shields him all day long, and the one the Lord loves rests between his shoulders."

– DEUTERONOMY 33:12, NIV

"This is real love – not that we have loved God, but that he loved us and sent his Son as a sacrifice to take away our sins."

– 1 JOHN 4:10, NLT

 Song: "Reckless Love" by Cory Asbury

Small Group – Session 6

<u>Loved</u>

1. If you already have a relationship with the Lord, try to remember the first time you met Him. Share with the group if you feel comfortable. If you don't yet have a relationship with Him and you want one, pray the prayer below with someone you are journeying with.

> ❖ *Dear Lord Jesus, I know that I am a sinner, and I ask for Your forgiveness. I believe You died for my sins and rose from the dead. I turn from my sins and invite You to come into my heart and life. I want to trust and follow You as my Lord and Savior. In Your Name. Amen.*

2. Are there any parts of you that have died internally? What needs to happen for you to feel alive again in this area?

3. Do you see prayer as another thing on your to-do list or a loving way to communicate with your Heavenly Father? How do you incorporate into your day?

4. If you're not doing so already, what is something you can do to invest in yourself? Do you see how crucial self-care is to your overall mindset?

5. Which love language do you identify with the most? Has anyone ever taken advantage of this or used it against you? If you find this memory still strikes a nerve, walk through the forgiveness process until you experience healing.

6. Have you experienced anything painful that might be holding you back from giving your heart fully to God? Do you believe how much He loves you? If you are struggling with this, I encourage you to pause and let the song Reckless Love play as you soak in the words. There's another list of love songs you can listen to in the Reference section. Consider it God's mixed tape to you.

7. What does love mean to you? Have you had life experiences that have altered your definition of love?

"Love is patient, love is kind. It does not envy, it does not boast, it is not proud. It does not dishonor others, it is not self-seeking, it is not easily angered, it keeps no record of wrongs. Love does not delight in evil but rejoices with the truth. It always protects, always trusts, always hopes, always perseveres."

                                            – 1 CORINTHIANS 13: 4-7, *NIV*

ENOUGH

. . .

Enough.

This is the word at the heart of my struggle. I often find myself people watching and wondering when I see couples, "What keeps them together? What made them decide that the other was enough for them to choose one another?" One of the worst things you can do is to compare yourself with others, but it happens. Even without thinking, it's automatic to let your mind drift there.

At the core of who we are, we all want to be enough to others. Whether it's our employer, parents, spouses, or children. We need to feel wanted and loved and important. The sad thing is that many of us feel like "enough" is a status we must reach, and then once that's accomplished, we stop trying. I've heard people say, "We're married, so he's stuck with me now." Not in this day and age when divorce has become such a common option.

The good news is that Jesus already settled it for us. He said we're enough, so much that He would die for us.

> *"But God showed His great love for us by sending Christ to die for us while we were still sinners."*
>
> *– ROMANS 5:8, NLT*

God didn't wait until we were perfect to make this sacrifice. He decided that we were enough right where we were. Sin in God's eyes is equal no matter how large or small. He didn't quantify in this verse that He died for only those who were basically good people. No, he died for the murderers, the thieves, the addicted and sexually immoral. Regardless of what your sin is, we are enough to Jesus.

"So God created mankind in his own image, in the image of God he created them; male and female he created them."

– GENESIS 1:27, NIV

This verse says it all. We are created in the image of the Almighty, Omniscient and Omnipotent Creator of this world. When God looked around at everything He created, He said "It is good." You are good. Regardless of your past or present mistakes, you carry the image of God inside of you. Even if you're not living like it, it's not too late to make some changes.

Even if that guy didn't make you feel good enough, you don't need a man to define your identity. You already have one.

"For we are God's handiwork, created in Christ Jesus to do good works, which God prepared in advance for us to do."

– EPHESIANS 2:10, NIV

We each have a purpose, so we must be important. God wouldn't create us if He didn't have a plan for our lives. But how will you know what the plan for your life is if you don't consult the One who prepared it? It would be like going to your child and asking what your boss needs you to do at work. If you want to know the truth, you must go direct to the source. We all know how the game of telephone turns out.

"I have told you these things, so that in me you may have peace. In this world you will have trouble. But take heart! I have overcome the world."

– JOHN 16:33, NIV

Not only are we enough for Jesus, but He is enough for us. Jesus has overcome the world. He is more than capable to help us with our problems. NOTHING is too great for Him!

"And my God will meet all your needs according to his glorious riches in Christ Jesus."

– PHILIPPIANS 4:19, NIV

Did you catch that? ALL of your needs. That settles it. You can't argue with that. It covers everything.

"Therefore, do not worry about tomorrow, for tomorrow will worry about itself. Each day has enough trouble of its own."

– MATTHEW 6:34, NIV

Don't we all know this to be true? But remember, this is where perspective comes into play. When we start feeling overwhelmed with our troubles, we have a choice. We can either meddle in our worries, or we can turn them over to God who promises to take care of us.

. . . .

Everything above is where I find my comfort. But I would only be telling you half the story if I didn't also share where I struggle.

Dating has only seemed to perpetuate my feelings of not being good enough. The first guy that I truly cared for after my divorce took me a long time to get over. I had fallen for him out of surprise actually and then was even more surprised when he seemed to have feelings for me in return. But forever feelings and lustful feelings are very different. Although he had presented many romantic gestures and flowery words in what I assumed was a display of "real" feelings, I had been fooled by what they call nowadays as "game."

It's sad really that what used to be a means to search for your life partner has now become a game of finding a quick Friday night fix. People aren't playing to win these days, they're just looking to advance to the next space and rent it for a weekend.

Initially, it seemed exciting to be able to date around and meet new people. Each person brought to the table different qualities to be admired. I knew I didn't want to settle this time. I had been through divorce once and knew what I was *not* looking for. The downside to dating around though is that when you take the positives of each person you meet and discard their flaws, you set the bar so high for the one you're saving yourself for that a real relationship seems almost unattainable. So many have given up trying to find a spouse and reduced dating to "just having fun." Get the best of everyone while settling for no one.

After I was divorced, I wrestled with whether abstinence outside of marriage still applied to me. I had been married and wasn't a virgin anymore, and so I needed to know if this changed God's advice to save sex for marriage. What I quickly figured out was this advice was not meant to punish us or keep us from having fun but more to protect us. Not only physically but also emotionally. The Bible tells us, *"Above all else, guard your heart, for everything you do flows from it." –PROVERBS 4:23, NIV*

For many people, sex carries an emotional attachment. As it should since God created sex for marriage, and we know that a man and a woman become one during this act of love. So, I couldn't guard my heart and also run around town creating an emotional web of ties to various men. The two are counterproductive.

What I found was when lustful passion entered the relationship too soon, it often caused other important relationship factors to take the backseat. Such as sharing the same values, having the same goals, etc. If you stay together long enough, you think, "we might as well get married," but often what happens is when hard times come, you don't have the foundation you need to withstand them and so many choose divorce.

Since Satan comes to steal, kill and destroy, this really seems like the perfect plan. Get people to buy into the mentality that they should live for whatever makes them happy. Have them run around town creating passionate memories of intense one-night stands that they will carry into their future, creating false expectations for their spouse to never live up to.

Once they have kids and realize that marriage is actually hard work, they decide it's not worth it and they give up. With each failed attempt at a relationship, hearts become hardened. The takeaway, whether they want to admit it or not is, "that wasn't enough for me," or even worse, "I wasn't enough."

Dating has become the black abyss of not knowing why you didn't make the cut. If you meet someone and go on a couple of dates, it's not like you can really fault them if they decide you're not a good fit. Although an explanation would be nice, I had to accept that they didn't owe me one. But being a part of a trial and error type of game isn't appealing to me. It hurts.

But the enemy wants us to question ourselves and our worth. As long as he can keep us in a tailspin of why we don't seem to measure up, then it becomes easy to not believe that God says we're enough. Why would God love us so much if nobody else wants to?

That's when we must raise our swords and use the Scripture mentioned above to fight back at the enemy and his attack on our value. Every time Jesus was confronted by the enemy, He fought back using God's word. We may be in this world, but we are not of this world, and our Heavenly Father did not leave us here without a plan to ensure we could find our way back to Him. He gave us everything we need in Him and His Word to be successful.

There have been many times over the last few years that I have said, "I have had *enough* of dating!" Honestly, it's exhausting to carry on small talk with someone for weeks and then have them disappear and have to start all over again. I have answered the question, "So where are you from?" at least a hundred times it seems. I'm not a small talk person either. I like deep conversations if I'm trying to get to know someone. It takes me a little bit to feel 100% comfortable sharing personal things but if a guy doesn't go past the surface level talk after a few weeks, it's not looking so promising.

I recently reconnected with a guy I used to "talk to" in grade school. I say "talk to" because we couldn't really date in the 4th/5th grades since we couldn't drive anywhere. Somewhere over the years we lost touch, and out of the blue he came to mind. So, I decided to look him up on Facebook. After scoping out his page to make sure he wasn't dating anyone, I decided to send him a message. We had quite a few conversations and even met up one night with some friends.

He told this story about how I was the first girl he told that he liked. We were at a school dance. He was in 5th grade. I was in 6th. I can't believe he remembered that! It was sweet. Something about having history feels safe and familiar. There was something about that familiarity that made me feel loved even for a second.

I tried really hard not to let myself think ahead and get my hopes up, but our conversations were so different from others I tried to have through online dating sites. Some guys just make it impossible to get to know them. I would get short answers with nothing to work with and it would often take hours or days between replies. I think the issue there is they weren't interested in getting to know me at all, they just wanted to know if I was interested in meeting up.

At the end of the night when we went out, he walked me to my car. If I was reading him correctly, there was a little nervousness in his voice as he asked if I'd like to do this again. I said yes of course and gave him my number to call me. I thought it was cute how he looked like a schoolboy again trying to gauge my interest.

But then a few weeks went by and he never asked for a date. He would reach out sometimes but not as much as I would like. He seemed interested when we talked, with long answers and engaging questions…but then nothing for days. I've learned the hard way over the years that if a guy is interested, he will pursue. You may get a few dates out of pursuing him, but it doesn't usually last.

I found this note I had scribbled in my notebook, "If you start off having to work for it, you'll never get far enough." The context of this isn't in regard to your career or to discourage your determination. I believe this spoke to me because it was talking about relationships. If a relationship is one-sided, one day when your efforts run dry, you will wake up and realize you are not being fulfilled. If you were to give up on the relationship, what would you have? Would they fight for you? Or are you the only one fighting?

I'm so ready to know who God has for me that sometimes I rush ahead. Have I met him yet? I don't want to lower my standards or settle, but I do want to be open to any possibility that God may present that I might initially overlook. But I have to watch myself so I don't get consumed down a one-track mindset and miss other things.

To sum up my dating life over the last few years, imagine picking up the latest and greatest romance novel that you can't wait to read. From the description on the back cover, it sounds perfect. You get a few chapters in and your mind is racing on how the story will develop. Right about the time when you're starting to know the characters and get excited for what happens next, you're forced to put the book down and stop reading. For various reasons, you don't get to know the ending. That's my love life right now. A shelf full of "what might have been."

There are many nights that I cry out to the Lord about how my heart aches to find the godly, family man that I'm searching for. I want so much for my son to grow up in a complete family the way God designed it to be. I want him to see the man being the spiritual leader of the home and providing for his family. To have a model of how a husband and wife should honor each other and always put love first.

I recently finished the show *Once Upon A Time*. I loved how the overarching theme throughout the entire show is HOPE. No matter what curses the enemy threw their way, they held onto the belief that love would win. Always. No matter what, you fight for it. You don't give up.

Love doesn't seem to hold the same value as it once did with earlier generations. Just tonight, I had a conversation with a friend who said she is so afraid to even attempt marriage because she sees the success rate of those around her. She was surprised to hear me say that I would marry again.

I refuse to let fear keep me from loving or being loved. I want to have a marriage that stands for something. I want to leave a legacy that inspires others to stick it out and work through their issues. Not because it's easy but because it's worth it.

. . . .

♪ *Song: "Take Courage" by Bethel Music*

Small Group – Session 7

Enough

1. Do you struggle with not feeling good enough? In what areas of your life does the guilt/shame weigh the heaviest?

2. Is it hard for you to accept that you were enough for Jesus to die for? Relish in that thought for a moment and whisper to yourself, "I am enough."

3. Is there an area where you struggle to believe that God will meet all of your needs?

4. Do you have a relationship in your life that is only one-sided? How can you restore the relationship so that both parties feel fulfilled?

5. Discuss how lustful passion can cause you to have rose colored glasses (defined as often thinking of something is better than it is) and not see things clearly?

6. If your group has singles currently in the dating season of life, talk about ways they can protect themselves from settling for people who don't share the same values/goals?

7. Are you waiting on God for anything? Pray together as a group for hope to cover this desire of your heart.

JEWELS ON MY JOURNEY

. . .

O nce I determined who I was in Christ, little rays of light began to shine through the darkness inside of my spirit. It didn't happen overnight. It didn't happen that year. It's been a process over the last seven years that is still continuing today. But as I look back in hindsight, I am amazed at God's faithfulness to carry us forward as we seek Him. I sit back in awe as I think about how broken I was compared to how content I feel today. I still don't have my happily ever after yet, but I have something to keep me going – HOPE.

After any tragedy or loss, it takes time to navigate the waves of emotions. This is completely normal. Even after I knew who I was, it didn't mean I never had days or moments that I didn't look in the mirror and not like who I saw. But the key is not to get stuck there. Every day is a new opportunity to be the best version of you.

"The steadfast love of the LORD NEVER CEASES; His mercies never come to an end; they are new every morning; great is your faithfulness."

– LAMENTATIONS 3: 22-23, ESV

Just because you had a painful season of life doesn't mean it's the end of your story. You may have gone through a divorce (fill in the blank with whatever has hurt you), but God has the final say. This is when He removes the period and replaces it with a comma. If you lean into Him and trust Him to guide you, He can rewrite your ending into His timeless masterpiece.

> *"I remain confident of this: I will see the goodness of the Lord in the land of the living. Wait for the Lord; be strong and take heart and wait for the Lord."*
>
> – PSALM 27: 13-14, NIV

All this time, I've been searching for how God would write my love story, but then I realized something – that's what He's been doing all along. From the moment I had that dream that I described in the Foreword. My mystery fiancé was Jesus!

> *"I will greatly rejoice in the Lord, My soul shall be joyful in my God; For He has clothed me with the garments of salvation, He has covered me with the robe of righteousness, As a bridegroom decks himself with ornaments, And as a bride adorns herself with her jewels."*
>
> – ISAIAH 61:10, NKJV

He adorned me with a beautiful, sparkly ring. He gave me everything I thought I was missing by not being physically married and so much more! Only once I started my journey with Him, did I realize that through Him, I had the **strength** and **provision** that I needed to **accept** what I could not change and **release** my bitterness so that I could **keep** my eyes fixed on Him and know that He says I am **loved** and **enough**.

Martin Luther King, Jr. once said, "Only in the darkness can you see the stars." While going through rough times is never enjoyable, in hindsight, we can often see how our darkest moments become our greatest victories.

Afterword

· · ·

B efore I close, I want to speak to those of you reading that are still married and looking for hope. Whether you're struggling with infidelity, addictions, financial hardships, etc., if BOTH of you are willing to do WHATEVER it takes to not give up and to look to God to help you through this valley, He *will* be faithful to see you through! You can't do this without Him though.

Ponder these questions with me for a minute before I tell you why.

- *Can I manage on one income?*
- *Can I watch my child cry himself to sleep at night because he misses his daddy?*
- *Will I have the sanity to handle everything on my own – every meal, housework, homework, discipline, etc.?*
- *How much do I like grilled food?*
- *Am I willing to power wash the house?*

When we struggle in our marriage, it's easy to look at our single friends and think they have the life. How fun it must be to go out on dates and just live it up. This has not been my experience at all! Do I enjoy having time to myself occasionally when my son is with his dad – yes…but would I trade that for all of the moments I miss out on his life that I can never get back – YES!!!

Dating…. honestly, I hate it. It's scary, awkward and not what it used to be! So there's two sides to every coin. Don't peer into someone else's life and wish it were yours until you have the full picture. Comparisons can be very dangerous. Take time to let your mind wander through the big picture, pros and cons, and not just the parts that sound exciting.

So back to the questions. There are probably two that stand out as weird, but I can explain. Grilled food. I love it! But I hate working the grill. We don't get along, and I have missing pieces of hair to prove it. The point of this question is just to think of something that you might miss if it was no longer in your life. It could be various different little things that get overlooked until they're gone. Maybe something you take for granted without realizing.

> I love the saying, *"Enjoy the little things in life…for one day you'll back and realize they were the big things."*
>
> -ROBERT BRAULT.

Power washing the house. Yardwork also falls into this category. What are things your spouse does that would fall onto your plate once you are living the single life? Funny story with power washing and a little about me. I hate reading directions. I would much rather have someone show me or tell me how to do something than have to read a manual. I generally glance through quickly and then give it a whirl. I often waste more time trying than if I would have stopped to read.

So the first time I go to power wash the house, I glance at the directions and I begin. I get the entire front of the house done, and I realize that although I had the water hose on and there was water coming out, I had not activated the cleaner because there was another setting labeled "Clean" that I had somehow missed. My arms were tired at this point, and I had already wasted thirty minutes. But once I tapped into the source, my job was so much easier. I still had to point the cleaner where I needed it to clean, but it did all of the work. Our power will only go so far. If you tap into the source, you gain access to abundant power.

When we try to live our lives on our own efforts, we often get frustrated, tired and burnt out when things don't go as planned. But what I've learned that I hope I conveyed in this book is that once we surrender every area of our life to God, we release His power into our lives. But both you and your spouse have to be on the same page with this. If one of you doesn't have your heart in it, the chances of success are slim. Can God use a wife's prayer to change things – I believe that He can, but there are two Scriptures that we can go to for this answer.

"And if a woman has a husband who is not a believer and he is willing to live with her, she must not divorce him. For the unbelieving husband has been sanctified through his wife, and the unbelieving wife has been sanctified through her believing husband."

– 1 CORINTHIANS 7: 13-14, NIV

"The person without the Spirit does not accept the things that come from the Spirit of God but considers them foolishness, and cannot understand them because they are discerned only through the Spirit."

-1 CORINTHIANS 2:14, NIV

If spouses are unequally yoked, God can still bless relationships because of the wife or husband. But I think the second verse puts into perspective why the success rate would be lower if both aren't on the same page.

My ex sat in some of the most powerful sermons when we were struggling, and I just knew that God would speak to him and change his heart if I could just get him in His Presence. But I was wrong. He wasn't in a place to receive any conviction from the Holy Spirit. His heart was so hardened by the guilt of his sin that nothing could penetrate. God's will cannot go where we are unwilling.

Remember, God looks at our hearts. We can pray all day long but if we don't have our hearts in it, our prayers will be hindered. Just like me hooking up the cleaner to the hose and not opening the release valve. It didn't work. But I promise, if both of your hearts are in it, and you tap into God's power, He will make your mess into something beautiful. He can wash any sin as white as snow.

. . . .

Other verses:

"I pray that God, the source of hope, will fill you completely with joy and peace because you trust in him. Then you will overflow with confident hope through the power of the Holy Spirit."

– ROMANS 15:13, NLT

"And this hope will not lead to disappointment. For we know how dearly God loves us, because he has given us the Holy Spirit to fill our hearts with his love."

– ROMANS 5:5, NLT

♪ *Song: "Never Stop" by SafetySuit*

FATHER'S LOVE LETTER
An intimate message from God to you.

My Child,

You may not know me, but I know everything about you. (1) I know when you sit down and when you rise up. (2) I am familiar with all your ways. (3) Even the very hairs on your head are numbered. (4) For you were made in my image. (5) In me you live and move and have your being. For you are my offspring. (6) I knew you even before you were conceived. (7) I chose you when I planned creation. (8)   You were not a mistake, for all your days are written in my book. (9) I determined the exact time of your birth and where you would live. (10)   You are fearfully and wonderfully made. (11) I knit you together in your mother's womb. (12)   And brought you forth on the day you were born. (13)   I have been misrepresented by those who don't know me. (14) I am not distant and angry, but am the complete expression of love. (15) And it is my desire to lavish my love on you.   Simply because you are my child and I am your Father. (16) I offer you more than your earthly father ever could. (17) For I am the perfect father. (18) Every good gift that you receive comes from my hand. (19)   For I am your provider and I meet all your needs. (20)   My plan for your future has always been filled with hope. (21)   Because I love you with an everlasting love. (22)   My thoughts toward you are countless as the sand on the seashore. (23)   And I rejoice over you with singing. (24)   I will never stop doing good to you. (25) For you are my treasured possession. (26)   I desire to establish you with all my heart and all my soul. (27) And I want to show you great and marvelous things. (28)   If you seek me with all your heart, you will find me. (29) Delight in me and I will give you the desires of your heart. (30)   For it is I who gave you those desires. (31) I am able to do more for you than you could possibly imagine. (32)   For I am your greatest encourager. (33) I am also the Father who comforts you in all your troubles. (34)   When you are brokenhearted, I am close to you. (35) As a shepherd carries a lamb, I have carried you close to my heart. (36)   One day I will wipe away every tear from your eyes. And I'll take away all the pain you have suffered on this earth. (37) I am your Father, and I love you even as I love my son, Jesus. (38) For in Jesus, my love for you is revealed. (39) He is the exact representation of my being. (40) He came to demonstrate that I am for you, not against you. (41)   And to tell you that I am not counting your sins. Jesus died so that you and I could be reconciled. (42)   His death was the ultimate expression of my love for you. (43) I gave up everything I loved that I might gain your love. (44)   If you receive the gift of my son Jesus, you receive me. (45) And nothing will ever separate you from my love again. (46)   Come home and I'll throw the biggest party heaven has ever seen. (47)   I have always been Father, and will always be Father. (48) My question is…Will you be my child? (49)   I am waiting for you. (50)

Love, Your Dad ...Almighty God

Father's Love Letter is a compilation of the following paraphrased Bible verses presented in the form of a love letter from God to you...
(1) Psalm 139:1; (2) Psalm 139:2; (3) Psalm 139:3; (4) Matthew 10:29-31; (5) Genesis 1:27; (6) Acts 17:28; (7) Jeremiah 1:4-5; (8) Ephesians 1:11-12; (9) Psalm 139:15-16; (10) Acts 17:26
(11) Psalm 139:14; (12) Psalm 139:13; (13) Psalm 71:6; (14) John 8:41-44; (15) 1 John 4:16; (16) 1 John 3:1; (17) Matthew 7:11; (18) Matthew 5:48; (19) James 1:17; (20) Matthew 6:31-33
(21) Jeremiah 29:11; (22) Jeremiah 31:3; (23) Psalm 139:17-18; (24) Zephaniah 3:17; (25) Jeremiah 32:40; (26) Exodus 19:5; (27) Jeremiah 32:41; (28) Jeremiah 33:3; (29) Deuteronomy 4:29
(30) Psalm 37:4; (31) Philippians 2:13; (32) Ephesians 3:20; (33) 2 Thessalonians 2:16-17; (34) 2 Corinthians 1:3-4; (35) Psalm 34:18; (36) Isaiah 40:11; (37) Revelation 21:3-4; (38) John 17:23
(39) John 17:26; (40) Hebrews 1:3; (41) Romans 8:31; (42) 2 Corinthians 5:18-19; (43) 1 John 4:10; (44) Romans 8:31-32; (45) 1 John 2:23; (46) Romans 8:38-39; (47) Luke 15:7
(48) Ephesians 3:14-15; (49) John 1:12-13; (50) Luke 15:11-32. © 1999 Father Heart Communications FathersLoveLetter.com - Please feel free to copy & share with others.

GOD'S MIXED TAPE TO YOU

· · ·

1. *How He Loves Us* by David Crowder Band
2. *You Say* by Lauren Daigle
3. *Make You Feel My Love* by Adele
4. *In My Arms* by Plumb
5. *Held* by Natalie Grant
6. *I Won't Let Go* by Rascal Flatts
7. *I Won't Let You Go* by Switchfoot/Lauren Daigle
8. *By Your Side* by Tenth Avenue North
9. *Rescue* by Lauren Daigle
10. *My Little Girl* by Tim McGraw
11. *Priceless* by For King and Country
12. *Beloved* by Tenth Avenue North
13. *My Wish* by Rascal Flatts

ACKNOWLEDGMENTS

. . .

E ach and every person in my life has played an important role in who I have become. From elementary teachers and childhood friends, my fond memories are not partial to the time that may have lapsed since I've seen some of you. If you know me, chances are I have a favorite memory of us that has shaped my life, no matter good or bad, and if I had the time, I would write to you all and thank you.

I have some of the best family and friends a girl could ever ask for! Words cannot even do justice for the gratitude I have toward my parents for always loving and supporting me and my son who has loved me no matter what. My church family has filled me with life and largely contributed to the advice in this book. They have guided my spiritual journey in ways that I will be forever grateful.

To the friends who read my story prior to publishing and offered their guidance and encouragement, I cannot thank you enough for taking the time out of your busy lives to make this all possible. And to my Single Women in Ministry group that agreed to be my guinea pigs, you're the best!

References

. . .

Eldredge, Stasi. *Becoming Myself.* Colorado Springs: David C Cook, 2013.

Furtick, Steven. *(UN)QUALIFIED: How God Uses Broken People to Do Big Things.* Colorado Springs: Multnomah Books, 2016.

Maner, Jessica. *To the pregnant women on social media posting constant updates and belly pictures, I am so incredibly happy for you and the fact that you will soon be blessed with the most amazing little bundle.* March 13, 2016. Used by permission. https://www.facebook.com/jessica.ward.1610/posts/919007301547879 (accessed April 24, 2019).

Moore, Beth. *Whispers of Hope: 10 Weeks of Devotional Prayer.* Nashville: B&H Publishing, 2013.

TerKeurst, Lysa. *Finding I Am: How Jesus Fully Satisfies the Cry of Your Heart.* Nashville: LifeWay Press, 2017.

CPSIA information can be obtained
at www.ICGtesting.com
Printed in the USA
LVHW091203281019
635557LV00001B/4/P

9 781400 325665